CHILDREN'S MINISTRY MAGAZINE'S BEST-EVER IDEAS

Group

Loveland, Colorado

Children's Ministry Magazine's Best-Ever Ideas

Credits
Thanks to all the authors who have contributed great ideas to CHILDREN'S MINISTRY Magazine over the years.
Book Acquisitions Editor: Mike Nappa
Editor: Susan L. Lingo
Compiler: Ann Marie Rozum
Senior Editor: Lois Keffer
Creative Products Director: Joani Schultz
Copy Editor: Amy Simpson
Art Director: Helen H. Lannis
Cover Art Director: Liz Howe
Designer: Helen H. Lannis
Computer Graphic Artist: Bill Fisher
Cover Designer: Rich Martin
Cover Photographer: Craig DeMartino
Illustrator: Gary Templin
Production Manager: Ann Marie Gordon

Unless otherwise noted, Scriptures quoted from The Youth Bible, New Century Version, copyright © 1991 by Word Publishing, Dallas, Texas 75039. Used by permission.

Library of Congress Cataloging-in-Publication Data
Children's ministry magazine's best ever ideas.
      p. cm.
    Includes index.
    ISBN 1-55945-623-X
     1. Christian education of children.   I. Children's ministry.
BV1475.2.C48   1996   95-47031
268'.432–dc20   CIP

10 9 8 7 6 5 4   05 04 03 02 01 00
Printed in the United States of America.
Visit our Web site: www.grouppublishing.com

CONTENTS

Creative Crafts

CONTENTS

Seasonal Ideas

CONTENTS

inTRODUCtiON

In a slump over worn-out games?
Stuck for a special craft?
Pondering ideas for Presidents' Day?

We have the perfect answers for you! Here are over 150 ideas for classroom crafts, games, and seasonal activities. These are not run-of-the-mill ideas but exciting, teacher-tested favorites from the pages of Group Publishing's CHILDREN'S MINISTRY Magazine. Since 1991, CHILDREN'S MINISTRY Magazine has had one goal: to provide the most exciting, unique, teacher-tested resources on the market. *Children's Ministry Magazine's Best-Ever Ideas* contains the cream of this crop—the most exciting games, the craftiest crafts, and the snappiest seasonal activities that make every day seem like a holiday. Included in this great collection are

- role-playing activities,
- cooperative games,
- lively songs,
- dynamic devotions,
- praise and worship ideas,
- crafts,
- edible art,
- small-group activities, and
- a handy index to help you choose the right activities for your children, from the nursery through upper elementary.

Children's Ministry Magazine's Best-Ever Ideas is more than just a book—it's a resource tool you'll use again and again to enliven your children's ministry and to give it sparkle.

So what are you waiting for? Dive into these pages for the best of the best in creative fun—you'll like what you see!

Great Games

• •

Adam's Animals

Best for early elementary
Supplies: You'll need a large box of animal crackers.

Choose a child to be Adam and have him or her stand at one end of the room. Gather the other children at the opposite end of the room. Help the children secretly pick an animal to imitate, such as a lion or a monkey. Have the children approach Adam, acting and sounding like the animal they've selected. When Adam calls out the name of the animal being imitated, have the children run back to the starting place while Adam tries to tag them. If someone is tagged, he or she becomes the next Adam.

For a different twist, let kids pick animal crackers and imitate the animals they pick.

After kids play a few times, hand each child a few animal crackers to enjoy. Encourage each child to tell about a pet or another animal he or she is thankful to God for creating.

All for One

Best for upper elementary
Supplies: none

Invite children to form groups of four. Say: **It's not always easy to agree with everyone—especially when you're in a big group. In this game, all the kids in your group must agree on one thing. For example, I'll ask what snack food you enjoy. Your group must find an answer you all agree on. If even one person doesn't agree, you must find another answer. Be careful— it's not as easy as it sounds!**

Read each of the following phrases aloud and allow time for each group to agree on an answer:

1. **something you like to do in the water**
2. **a snack food you like to eat**
3. **a story of Jesus you like**
4. **a subject in school you like**
5. **a place you like to go for fun**
6. **a holiday you enjoy**
7. **a sport you enjoy playing or watching**
8. **a TV program you enjoy**

Ask:

● **Which statements were hardest to agree on?**
● **What was the most surprising thing you agreed on?**
● **What did you learn about each other?**

Say: **It's not always easy to agree on everything, but I liked the way you respected each other's answers! It's good that God made all of us special and with equally good ideas.**

Balloon Relay

Best for early and upper elementary
Supplies: You'll need balloons, a ruler, and masking tape.

Before the game, place a 4-foot piece of masking tape on the floor across one end of the classroom. Form teams of four to six children. Have teams line up in rows at the end of the room opposite the tape line.

Hand each player a balloon. Say: **Let's have a wacky race with our balloons. The first player in each line will blow up the balloon but won't tie it. The players will aim their balloons toward the finish line at the other end of the room then let their balloons go. Watch where the balloons land! The next players in line will run to where the balloons landed then blow up their balloons and let them go. We'll see whose balloon crosses the finish line first, then we'll start again!**

The first team to have all players cross the finish line wins.

Bellybutton Buddies

Best for nursery and preschool
Supplies: none

Even your youngest players will adore this silly game! Gather children in a circle and say: **Can you point to your bellybutton?** Pause for kids to respond. **Let's play a funny game called Bellybutton Buddies. We'll hop around the room. When I say "bellybuttons," find a friend and point to his or her bellybutton. Then we'll hop again.**

If you have very young toddlers in your class, have them point to their own bellybuttons. Older preschoolers love this game when they each get a turn to be the caller. For extra fun, have kids point to their elbows, heads, arms, or toes instead of their bellybuttons!

Bible Olympics

Best for upper elementary
Supplies: You'll need to gather a variety of objects for these fast-paced games that are Olympic-sized fun! Read the directions for each game below to determine the supplies you'll need.

Get your kids to "go for the gold" with this event. Set up three or more of the following events:

● **Race to Jerusalem**—Have kids race barefoot around a masking tape course on stick horses with paper donkey-ears.

● **Bibliathon**—Write the name of each book of the Bible on a tongue depressor, then let kids race to put the names in the correct order!

● **David vs. Goliath**—Invite kids to hurl large marshmallows at a "shield" target made from a trash-can lid or from paper plates covered with aluminum foil.

● **Feeding the 5,000**—In this event, kids race to tear the most pieces from flour tortillas.

● **Strong as Samson?**—Let kids pull a heavy object such as a trash can attached to a rope.

● **Noah Needs Help**—Let kids see how many stuffed animals they can move from one box to another without using their hands.

● **Happy Birthday, Jesus**—Invite kids to "extinguish" a paper-candle flame with a water gun.

● **Goin' Fishin'**—Let kids "fish" for paper fish. Put paper clips on paper fish, then tie a string on a stick and attach a magnet to the end of the string.

For extra fun, give a blue ribbon to everyone who participates in the events!

Bible Smuggle

Best for early and upper elementary
Supplies: You'll need a Bible.

Have kids stand in a large circle, holding their hands behind their backs. Choose someone to stand in the center of the circle. Hold up the Bible and say: **Let's see how clever you are at passing the Bible without letting the person in the center know where the Bible is. We'll pass the Bible behind our backs for a few seconds, then we'll see if the person in the center can guess where it is.** Have kids begin passing the Bible behind their backs around the circle. Encourage kids to try to confuse the person in the center so he or she doesn't know where the Bible is. Kids can *pretend* to pass the Bible back and forth.

After 30 seconds, have the center person guess who's holding the Bible. If the guess is correct, the person holding the Bible becomes the next center person. If the guess is incorrect, have the kids continue passing the Bible. Play this game until children tire of it.

Then say: **In some countries, it's against the law to have a Bible, so Christians smuggle the Bible into these countries. Many people risk their lives so others can have Bibles.** Ask:

● **How did you feel when the Bible came into your hands?**
● **What would you do if it were against the law to have a Bible?**
● **Why is the Bible important to Christians?**

This is a great game for reviewing Bible stories. Instead of having kids repeat verses, have them answer questions about Bible stories they've learned.

Bible-Verse Volleyball

Best for upper elementary
Supplies: You'll need a Bible, a long table, a chalkboard, and balloons.

Use this active game to perk up your work on Scripture verses.

Write a Bible verse on the chalkboard. Have kids form two groups, and have them stand on opposing sides of a long table. Blow up and tie off a balloon.

Say: **There's nothing as fun as a good game of volleyball. Let's play balloon volleyball for even more fun! We'll bop this balloon ball back and forth across the table. If the balloon touches the ground, the group that let it touch must repeat the Bible verse on the chalkboard. Then I'll erase one word from the verse. We'll keep playing until one group says the entire verse with no words on the chalkboard to help!**

Toss the balloon into the air to begin the game. When the game is over, write another verse on the chalkboard and play again. Use this exciting game whenever you want to motivate kids to work on verse repetition.

Body Language

Best for early elementary
Supplies: none

This fun letter game will thrill your kids! Have children form teams or have them work together in one large group.

Call out a letter of the alphabet. Have children lie on the floor and work together to form that letter. Every child should be part of the letter—no bystanders! Older kids will enjoy this extra challenge: Let kids suggest biblical words, people, or phrases to form with their arms, legs, and bodies. You might also have kids spell out the words to memory verses you've been working on. Kids love this new twist on Scripture memory!

Bouncing Balloon

Best for early and upper elementary
Supplies: You'll need index cards, markers, and a balloon.

Before this game, number 10 index cards from one to 10. Draw a shape on each of five additional index cards. Blow up a balloon and tie it.

Have kids stand close together in a group. Mix the cards and lay them face down in two piles: one for the numbered cards and one for the cards with shapes. Give one child the balloon and have another child turn over a card from each pile and call out the number and the shape.

Have kids begin bopping the balloon around the group. Have them keep the balloon in the air for the number of hits designated on the number card while they name things that have the shape on the shape card. For example, if the number card shows a two and the shape card shows a circle, the first child will hit the balloon and call out "one" and the name of something shaped like a circle: "One, wheel." A second child will hit the balloon and say something like "Two, balloon."

The last child to hit the balloon catches it then turns over another card from each pile to start the game again.

Christmas-Cookie Relay

Best for early and upper elementary
Supplies: You'll need masking tape, two cookie sheets, construction paper, two spatulas, scissors, and a box of small Christmas cookies.

Before this activity, cut cookie shapes from construction paper. Cut out shapes such as stars, hearts, flowers, and gingerbread men. Be sure there's a paper cookie for each child.

Divide the paper cookies between two cookie sheets, then place the cookie sheets at one end of the room. Have kids form two lines behind a line of masking tape at the opposite end of the room. Hand the first person in each line a spatula.

On "go," have the first person in each line walk backward to the cookie sheet, scoop a paper cookie onto his or her spatula, then hop back without dropping the cookie. If a cookie falls, have the player scoop it up and continue.

When everyone has had a turn to scoop up a cookie, let each player turn in his or her paper cookie for a *real* Christmas-cookie treat!

> **T·I·P**
>
> **For festive fun, let kids decorate sugar cookies with canned icing and sparkly sprinkles!**

Classroom Trivia

Best for upper elementary
Supplies: You'll need colored index cards and a Trivial Pursuit game board.

Make a "classroom trivia" board game to help kids in your class get to know each other better. Before class, interview each child. You can ask kids for their favorites, not-so-favorites, and best memories regarding family, friends, food, school, and hobbies.

Ask questions such as "What's your favorite food?" "When is your favorite time of day?" and "What is your least favorite thing about school?"

Use this information to make game cards. Write the information for each child on colored index cards, using a different color of card for each category. Use red for family cards, blue for food cards, yellow for friends, green for school cards, and white for hobbies. On one card you might write, "This person hates hamburgers but could take a bath in pistachio ice cream" or "While playing touch football one afternoon, this person broke an ankle."

Use a Trivial Pursuit game board to play, following the regular rules of the game. Kids will enjoy the game and everyone will be a winner as kids get to know each other better.

Creation in Motion

Best for preschool
Supplies: none

Have kids spread out and sit down on the floor. If your room has windows that let in light, turn off the overhead lights. Say: **We know that God made everything in the world. He made trees and sunshine and water and animals and each of us, too! Let's act out the days God created the world and everything in it.** Paraphrase the story from Genesis 1:1–2:3 as children do these actions after each day's description: Day 1—turn the lights on and stand up; Day 2—raise their hands and form imaginary clouds. Then sway back and forth to imitate ocean waves; Day 3—pat the ground and pretend to pick flowers; Day 4—hold their arms in large circles over their heads; Day 5—make flying motions like birds, then lay on their tummies and pretend to swim like fish; Day 6—Imitate animals of their choice; Day 7—lie on the floor and rest.

After the story, lead children in saying, "God looked at everything he had made, and it was very good." Clap and cheer and thank God for creating the world!

Crepe Paper Praise

Best for preschool
Supplies: You'll need 3-foot streamers of brightly colored crepe paper, a cassette player, and a cassette tape of lively children's music.

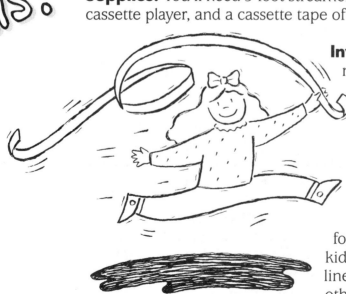

Invite children to praise God with music and motion.

Give each child a 3-foot streamer to wave and twirl in time to praise music such as "Lord of the Dance" or "Joyful, Joyful, We Adore Thee." Encourage children to think of how happy they feel knowing God loves them.

Get kids excited about praising by forming a long "praise line." Have kids take turns being the Leader of the line and waving their streamers for the others to follow.

Feather Fun Catch

Best for early elementary
Supplies: You'll need a feather and animal stickers (at least two of each animal).

Your kids will be tickled by this fun feather-tossing game! Invite kids to sit in a circle on the floor. Place an animal sticker on one hand of each child. Hold the feather and stand in the center of the circle. Say: **Let's have some animal fun. I'll toss this feather high in the air and call out the name of an animal. If you're wearing that animal sticker, hop up and try to catch the feather before it lands on the floor. If you catch the feather, you can have the next turn tossing it and calling out the name of another animal. If no one is able to catch the feather, we'll toss it again.**

Play until everyone has had a turn to toss the feather.

For an exciting variation, have kids make the appropriate animal sounds as they rush to catch the feather. You may wish to toss two feathers at one time.

Follow Me

Best for preschool
Supplies: You'll need a bright flashlight and a bandanna or scarf for each pair of kids.

Kids have "twice the fun" in this partner game and learn lots about God!

Gather kids and say: **The Bible tell us that God is light. And God wants us to follow him. We can play a fun game with partners and follow the light.**

Help kids get with partners, then use the bandanna or scarf to gently tie each person's leg to his or her partner's leg as in a three-legged race. Say: **I'll turn off the lights then shine a flashlight around the room. See if you and your partner can follow the light.** Shine the flashlight around the room, allowing the light to stay in one place for a few seconds before moving it to a new location. Encourage partners to help each other follow the light.

After the game, untie the children's legs. Invite kids to sit in a circle. Ask:
● **What was it like following the light?**
● **How did you help your partner?**

Say: **We can help each other follow God by praying for each other and by going to church together. Let's pray and ask God to help us follow him.** Close in prayer.

Friendship Circle

Best for early elementary
Supplies: You'll need one plastic hoop, two large jars, table tennis balls, and a permanent marker.

This game is a real esteem-builder for kids—and they'll love the crazy ball they'll get to take home!

Before the game, write each child's name on a table tennis ball, using a permanent marker. You may want to add small decorations such as hearts, stars, flowers, or polka-dots. Place the table tennis balls in a large jar.

Set the plastic hoop on the floor in the center of the room and invite kids to sit around the hoop. Place the jar containing the table tennis balls and the empty jar in the center of the circle.

Say: **This is our friendship circle, and there are many names in this circle. I'll choose someone to step into the circle and pull a table tennis ball from the jar. You can read the name on the ball aloud then invite the person with that name into the friendship circle with you. You may tell that person one good thing about him or her, such as "I like your smile" or "You're always ready to help people." Then that person may draw out a table tennis ball.**

Continue until everyone has been in the friendship circle. Be sure to let the kids take home their table tennis balls as happy reminders of their affirmations.

God's Colorful Creations

Best for early elementary
Supplies: You'll need a Bible, colorful construction paper, a ruler, a chalkboard or a large sheet of paper, scissors, tape, and chalk or markers.

Before class, cut 1-inch squares of colorful construction paper. Cut one square for each child.

As children arrive, tape a colored square to each person's back without letting that person see the color. Tell kids not to reveal any of the colors to each other.

Gather kids in a circle on the floor and choose one person to stand with his or her back to the group. Encourage the group to call out items that are the same color as the square on the child's back. When the child guesses the correct color, he or she may sit down.

As kids call out items, write them on a chalkboard or a large sheet of paper. After everyone has had a turn to guess the color, ask kids to put check marks by the listed items that God created. Read aloud Colossians 1:16 and end your game by tossing the colored squares in the air and saying, "Thank you, God, for everything!"

Heart-Stopping Stories

Best for upper elementary
Supplies: You'll need a bag of candy conversation hearts.

To prepare for this storytelling game, either invent a story beforehand or read a familiar fairy tale. If you're feeling especially creative, you might even ad-lib this activity!

Ask the children to sit in a circle, and give each child 10 candy conversation hearts with sayings on them. Recite your story, stopping at times so kids have a chance to complete your sentences with candy-heart sayings. For example, you might say, "When the wolf saw the sheep, it said . . ." A child might complete your sentence by saying, "Wow" or "Will you be mine?"

Let each child tell his or her saying then gobble the candy hearts while you continue the story.

T·I·P

If you have a large group, let kids sit in pairs and read the heart sayings to each other instead of sitting in the circle.

Hearty Beanbag Zoo

Best for preschool and early elementary
Supplies: You'll need nature magazines, red construction paper, scissors, tape, and a beanbag.

Before this activity, cut a red construction paper heart for each child. Cut animal pictures from nature magazines and tape an animal picture to each heart. Tape the hearts face down to the floor and set a beanbag near the hearts. If you don't have beanbags, make them in a snap by pouring dried beans into kids' socks then knotting the ankles.

Let one child at a time toss a beanbag onto the hearts. Gently untape the heart closest to the beanbag, and invite the child to imitate the animal pictured on that heart. Invite the other kids to guess the name of the animal then to join in making the appropriate animal sounds.

Continue playing until every child has had a turn to toss the beanbag and act out an animal.

T·I·P

If time permits, allow children to search through magazines for animal pictures.

Hoop Shoop

Best for preschool through upper elementary
Supplies: You'll need plastic hoops or large loops of yarn.

Have kids form groups of five, and hand each group a plastic hoop or a large loop of yarn. Choose one player in each group to be the "tagger." Have the tagger stand in the center of the plastic hoop or the loop of yarn. Have the other four players stand outside the hoop and hold it around the edges.

Say: **The object of this game is to keep from being touched on the hand by the tagger in the center of the hoop. You may hold the hoop with only one**

one hand at a time and must keep alternating hands to keep from being tagged. If you're tagged, you become the new tagger. For a real challenge with older kids, blindfold the tagger!

It's Easter!

Best for early elementary
Supplies: You'll need one plastic Easter egg for each child, a basket, a cassette player, a musical cassette tape of your choice, and a sticker.

Before this activity, attach the sticker inside one of the plastic Easter eggs. Ask children to form a circle, then give everyone a plastic egg. Designate one wall as "home base." Set the basket off to one side of the playing area.

Say: **Let's play a game to remind us how the angels told Jesus' friends that Jesus was alive that first Easter morning. Pass your eggs around the circle in time to the music. When the music stops, open the egg you're holding. The person who has the sticker inside his or her egg can shout, "It's Easter!" Then that person will try to tag us before we make it to home base. If you're tagged, put your egg in the basket, then you can help tag kids on the next round.**

For extra excitement, have kids reverse the direction they're passing the eggs.

Light the Way

Best for nursery, preschool, and early elementary
Supplies: You'll need a working flashlight.

Gather children at one end of the room while you stand at the opposite end with a working flashlight. Say: **Let's play a game of light and dark. I'll shine the flashlight. When you see the light, tiptoe toward me. But when I turn the light off, stop! We'll see if you can make it all the way to where I'm standing!**

Alternately turn the flashlight off and on. When kids reach you, let them touch the flashlight then return to play again. If you have older kids, turn out the lights for extra fun. You may wish to let older preschoolers and elementary kids be flashlight holders for some games.

When you're finished playing, say: **Sometimes the dark can be scary. But just as this flashlight helped us find our way, Jesus helps us feel safe when we're afraid. Jesus is always with us, lighting the way! Let's clap and cheer for Jesus!**

Lost Coins

Best for preschool and early elementary
Supplies: You'll need a Bible, newspaper, and pennies.

Kids love to play Hide-and-Seek, and this game will give the old favorite a new twist! Hand each child two sheets of newspaper and tell kids to crumple the paper and make a pile of paper wads. Have kids hide their eyes while you toss a few pennies into the paper wads. If you're playing with preschool children, hide larger things such as blocks. Let kids search for the lost items. When they find the items, encourage kids to cheer and clap. Pile up the paper wads again and have the children who found the items hide them. Play until everyone has had a chance to hide the objects.

After all the coins have been found or children tire of this game, read aloud the parable of the lost coin from Luke 15:8-10. Encourage kids to tell about times they've lost then found important things and how they felt.

Lucky Guess

Best for preschool
Supplies: You'll need a box of Lucky Charms cereal, three empty bowls, and a table.

Have children guess how many marshmallow hearts are in half a box of Lucky Charms cereal. After each child has guessed, place three empty bowls on a table—one bowl for marshmallow hearts, one for other marshmallow shapes, and one for the rest of the cereal.

Give each child a scoop of cereal to sort into the appropriate bowls. Then help the children count the marshmallow hearts in the bowl to see whose guess came closest. Celebrate great counting and teamwork by sharing the remaining cereal.

T·I·P

Use the cereal you counted to make a pretty mosaic. Let kids glue cereal and colorful marshmallow bits to paper plates, craft sticks, or paper cups.

23

Magnetic Personalities

Best for early elementary
Supplies: none

Gather kids at one end of the playing area and say: **We know that magnets attract paper clips and pins and other metals. Let's have some fun pretending to be magnets. I'll call out a description that might fit you. If that description does fit you, hop to the center of the room and form a tight circle with the other "magnets." Let's try that once. Everyone wearing blue jeans, hop to the center.** Pause while kids wearing blue jeans form a tight circle, then have them return to their places.

Here are some suggestions for descriptions:
- everyone wearing blue socks,
- everyone wearing stripes,
- everyone who has two eyes,
- everyone who likes ice cream,
- everyone who likes spinach, and
- everyone who knows how to drive a real car.

For extra fun, let kids take turns being the caller and making up descriptions.

My Favorite Things

Best For upper elementary
Supplies: none

Have the children stand in the middle of the room.

Say: **I'm going to read a list of categories. Each time I name a category, call out your favorite thing in that category. Keep calling it out until you find other people who have the same favorite. For example, if I say "movie," you might call out, *"The Lion King."* Everyone who is calling out the same movie can form a group. If you're the only one with that favorite, that's fine! You're a unique person!**

Here are some suggestions for categories you may wish to call: food, music, color, movie, sport, season, and subject in school. You may wish to let each child call out a category.

After you've called out five categories, say: **All of us may like different things, but that's the way God made us. We're all special!**

Noah's Ark

Best for nursery and preschool
Supplies: none

Have kids form a circle, and tell them they're going to sing about the animals on Noah's ark. Lead kids in singing the following words to the tune of "Old MacDonald Had a Farm":

Mister Noah had an ark.
O-ee-o-ee-o!
And on this ark he had two frogs.
O-ee-o-ee-o!
With a ribbit here and a ribbit there;
Here a ribbit, there a ribbit—everywhere a ribbit, ribbit.
Mister Noah had an ark.
O-ee-o-ee-o!

Have kids imitate the animals as they sing. For example, have kids hop around like frogs while they say "ribbit."

Each time kids sing the song, change the animal and the noise. For extra active fun, do motions to accompany the animal sounds. For elephants, use your arms as swaying trunks; make scratching motions for monkeys; and wiggle like swimming fish.

If you have toddlers in your room, hold up pictures of animals and let children name the animals and make the appropriate animal sounds.

Red-Hot Fun

Best for upper elementary
Supplies: You'll need small cinnamon candies, toothpicks, and paper cups.

Ask kids to form pairs, and hand each pair a paper cup. Have pairs place their paper cups on the floor at one end of the room then stand at the opposite end. Give each pair 15 small cinnamon candies and four toothpicks. Say: **Set your candies on the floor in front of you. Be sure you and your partner each have two toothpicks. When I say "go," you'll have two minutes to transfer all your candies into your paper cups at the other end of the room. You might roll the candies or carry them on your toothpicks, but no hands allowed! You'll really have to work together!**

At the end of two minutes, have kids count the candies in their cups. Let the kids with the most cinnamon candies line up first for drinks of water. Talk about how much easier the game was when partners worked together. Be sure everyone gets a few fresh cinnamon candies to eat!

T·I·P

Give this game holiday zip by using seasonal treats such as jelly beans, candy hearts, peppermints, or candy corn.

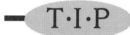

T·I·P

Try this for some extra-zany fun: Hand each child a paper wad and let him or her pass it in some crazy way to the next player in line. Encourage kids to imitate the way the paper wads were passed to them as they continue passing the paper wads up and down their lines!

Roundabout Relay

Best for early and upper elementary
Supplies: You'll need white paper and colored paper.

Before this game, make a wad from white paper and one from colored paper. Form two groups and have the groups line up across from each other. Give the person in the front of each line a white paper wad. Hand the person at the back of each line a colored paper wad.

Say: **This is a zany game of passing paper wads. The white paper wads will be passed through your legs, while the colored paper wads will be passed over your heads. We'll see if your group can pass both paper wads at once without getting all mixed up!**

On "go," have the first player in each line pass the white paper wad through his or her legs to the next player in line. Have the last player in line pass the colored paper wad overhead to the player in front of him or her. Have kids continue passing the paper wads up and down the lines until both paper wads return to their original positions.

Samaritan Shuffle

Best for upper elementary
Supplies: You'll need a Bible, a pencil, balloons, a wastebasket, and slips of paper.

T·I·P

Play this hoppin', poppin' game to review any Bible story you've been learning!

Before the game, write each of the following events from the story of the Good Samaritan (Luke 10:30-37) on a slip of paper.
● A man walks from Jerusalem to Jericho.
● Robbers attack and beat up the man.
● A priest walks past the wounded man.
● A Levite walks past the wounded man.
● A Samaritan stops to bandage the man's wounds.
● A Samaritan puts the wounded man onto an animal.
● A Samaritan takes the wounded man to a motel.
● A Samaritan pays the motel manager to take care of the hurt man.

Put each slip of paper into a different balloon. Inflate and tie off the balloons. Gather kids in a circle. Hold up the balloons and say: **Let's play a fun review of the story of the Good Samaritan. These balloons contain parts to the story. We'll bop balloons back and forth. When I say, "Stop and pop!" snatch a balloon and sit on it until the balloon pops. Then read the slip of paper that was inside. We'll see if we can fit the parts of the story together.**

After kids have popped their balloons, help them "reassemble" the Bible story, then read it aloud. Then ask a volunteer to read aloud Luke 10:30-37.

Say: **It's time to be good Samaritans, so let's help each other clean up the room and toss the popped balloons in the wastebasket.**

Scavenger Hunt

Best for upper elementary
Supplies: You'll need Bibles, paper, markers, and a copy of the "Scavenger List" handout (p. 28).

Have kids form pairs or trios, and hand each person a "Scavenger List" handout and a marker. Let kids work together to complete items one through 11. Then gather everyone into a group to finish item 12.

See and Say

Best for preschool
Supplies: You'll need magazines, scissors, index cards, and tape.

Before this activity, cut out of magazines pictures of things such as animals, musical instruments, cars, and other objects that make noise. Tape the pictures to index cards.

Have kids sit in a circle, and place the pictures face down in a pile in the center. Let children take turns drawing a card and holding it up for everyone to see. Ask questions about the pictures, such as "What is this?" "What sound does it make?" and "How does it move?" Let children respond in unison with noises and motions.

For a more elaborate game, cut a large circle from poster board and divide the circle into pie-shaped wedges. Tape a picture to each pie-shaped section of the circle. Attach an arrow-shaped spinner to the center of the circle with a paper fastener. Have kids take turns spinning the arrow instead of drawing a card.

Shoo, Fly!

Best for early and upper elementary
Supplies: You'll need a Bible.

Gather kids at one end of the playing area. Say: **Sometimes we think we know what other people are feeling or thinking. Let's play a game to see what it's like to be in someone else's place! Find a partner, then trade shoes with that person.** Pause for children to put on each other's shoes as best they can.

Say: **When I say, "Shoo, fly!" walk backward to the other side of the room and back.**

After everyone has finished, have kids switch back to their own shoes. While they put on their shoes, say: **A well-known saying says, "Don't judge another person until you've walked a mile in his or her shoes." What do you think this means? How easy was it to walk in someone else's shoes?**

(continued on p. 29)

Scavenger List

1. ■ Draw a picture of the animal in Luke 22:60.

2. ■ Find something the color of the things people carried in John 12:13.

3. ■ Put your resources together or borrow to collect the number of coins in Matthew 26:15.

4. ■ Find a small version of the item in Mark 16:4.

5. ■ Draw a picture of the body part in Luke 22:50.

6. ■ Get the same thing the man was carrying in Mark 14:13.

7. ■ Make a paper version of what the soldiers made for Jesus in John 19:2.

8. ■ Locate something the color of the robe in Mark 15:17.

9. ■ Make a sign like the one in Matthew 27:37.

10. ■ Draw what the soldier used in John 19:34.

11. ■ Tear out of paper a model of the items in Mark 14:22 and Luke 22:17.

12. ■ Have each team member tell what Jesus' death and resurrection means to him or her.

(continued from p. 27)

Read aloud Matthew 7:1-5. Ask:
- **What does it mean to judge someone?**
- **What does this passage say about judging?**
- **Why do you think God doesn't want us to judge others?**
- **How can we "walk a mile" in someone else's shoes?**

Close by reading aloud Romans 15:7.

Solar System Spin

Best for upper elementary
Supplies: You'll need chairs.

Place chairs in a large circle and invite kids to sit down. Designate each child as one of the nine planets: Mercury, Venus, Earth, Mars, Jupiter, Saturn, Uranus, Neptune, or Pluto. You must have more than one child representing each planet.

Have one child be the "satellite" and stand in the center of the circle. Say: **I see lots of planets in our room, but will they stay in the same orbiting path? Not if the satellite has its way! The satellite will call out the name of a planet. Anyone with that planet name can jump up, spin around once, then find a different seat before the satellite finds a place to sit. The planet left without a seat becomes the next satellite!**

Play until everyone has had a chance to be the satellite.

Spin-a-Hug

Best for nursery and preschool
Supplies: You'll need poster board, markers, and a beanbag.

Before playing, make a game board by drawing a heart for each child in class on a sheet of poster board. Write each child's name on a separate heart. If you don't have a beanbag, make one by pouring dried beans into a child's sock then knotting the ankle.

Set the heart game board on the floor and gather kids a few feet away. Have them take turns tossing the beanbag onto the game board. Each time the beanbag lands on the game board, read aloud the name closest to the beanbag. The child who tossed the beanbag can hug the child whose name was called.

Continue until everyone has had at least one hug. Play again, but use "love pats" instead of hugs.

Spread the Word

Best for upper elementary
Supplies: You'll need a Bible, a pencil, a globe, and slips of paper.

Before the kids arrive, write Scripture references on slips of paper. Use familiar verses such as John 3:16, Romans 3:23, and Ephesians 2:8. Be sure you have a verse for each child.

Tell kids they'll play a relay game using Bible verses that they can tell to the whole world.

Hand each child a slip of paper with a verse on it. Have kids form two lines at one end of the room. Place a globe at the opposite end of the room.

Say: **Let's play a game to remind us how important it is to tell God's Word around the world. When I say "go," the first player in each line will run to the globe at the other end of the room. Touch the globe while you read the Scripture reference on your paper, then hop back and tap the next person in your line so he or she can tell God's Word around the world.**

When everyone has had a turn, ask volunteers to look up the verses in the Bible and read them aloud. Ask questions such as "Why does God want us to spread his Word?" and "Who is one person you can tell about God this week?"

Stalking Goliath

Best for early and upper elementary
Supplies: You'll need two scarves and a table.

Kids will enjoy playing this fun hunting game.

Before playing, remove all the chairs from the playing area. Help kids get with partners, and have them play this game one pair at a time. Use the scarves to blindfold the first pair, and have the partners stand on either side of a table, each with one hand on the table. Designate one partner as Goliath and the other as David. Have the rest of the kids sit a few feet away from the table, and encourage them to cheer for the kids playing.

Say: **Goliath's job is to keep away from David. David's job is to catch Goliath. You may travel around the table in either direction as long as you keep one hand on the table at all times. We'll see who catches who in this game of hunt and chase!**

Kids who are watching will have fun, but tell them not to give any clues. Have kids play until David catches Goliath or for one minute. Then let another pair play.

Sticky-Glue Tag

Best for preschool
Supplies: none

Say: Having good friends is a lot of fun. Let's play a game about sticking close to our friends. I'll choose someone to be the "glue." Don't let the glue tag you, or you'll be stuck to him or her. If you're tagged, hold hands with the glue and help tag others. We'll play until everyone is "stuck" together!

As each child is tagged, be sure he or she holds hands with the last person in line. Continue playing until all the kids are joined together. If time permits, choose another child or pair of kids to be the glue, and play again. Then gather the kids in a circle and ask:

● What was it like to tag people when lots of friends helped?
● How can friends help each other every day?

Encourage kids to tell things about their friends, such as what they like to do together, where their friends live, or their friends' names.

Strength in Numbers

Best for early and upper elementary
Supplies: You'll need a Bible and a whistle.

Gather kids into a group and choose one child to be the "caller." Designate a "safety zone" at one side of your playing area.

Say: **It's fun to play in a group, and in this game we'll make lots of groups of different sizes. When I say "mix-up," hop around until you hear the whistle blow. Then the caller will call out a number between two and five. Run to form groups of that number before you're tagged by the caller. If you're left without a group, run to the safety zone, where you can't be tagged. The first person tagged becomes the next caller.**

After kids play this game several times, have them sit down for a breather. Ask a volunteer to read aloud Ecclesiastes 4:9-12. Ask:

● What do you think this verse is saying about needing people to help us?
● How can having friends help you be strong in your faith?
● What are ways we can help each other at school? home? church?

Tail Chase

Best for early and upper elementary
Supplies: You'll need a Bible and bandannas.

Have kids form groups of five. Instruct each group to stand in a line so that each person's hands are on the waist or the shoulders of the next person in line. Have the last player in each line tuck a bandanna into his

or her pocket or waistband so it hangs out like a tail.

Say: **How about a great game of chase? The first person in each line will try to snatch the tail from the last player. But there's one big catch: The people in the middle can keep the tail from being snatched! If your line comes apart, you must sit down until the next round.**

Play the game a few times, then form new groups so kids have an opportunity to participate with different people. Be sure to switch line leaders and "tail ends."

After the game, read Philippians 2:1-2 aloud. Ask kids to explain how the game illustrated the verses. Ask questions such as "How does it help when people working together agree on what they're working on?" and "What's it like to work with someone you don't agree with?" Invite kids to tell about times they have worked with other people.

Tattle "Tails"

Best for early and upper elementary
Supplies: You'll need a Bible, hinge-type clothespins, and markers.

Set out hinge-type clothespins and markers. Invite kids to write their names on clothespins. Then have kids clip the clothespins to the backs of their shirts.

Say: **These are "tails," and your goal is to capture other players' tails without losing yours. Chase each other until all the tails are captured.**

Afterward, read aloud Genesis 37:2. Ask:

● **What does it mean that Joseph brought "bad reports" about his brothers?**

● **What do we call people who tell on others a lot?**

Say: **Joseph was a tattletale. But tattling often makes us and others feel bad. Let's do something new—let's be *good* tattletales! For each clothespin tail you snatched, say one good thing about the person whose name is on it.**

Continue until everyone has been affirmed.

Trading Places

Best for early and upper elementary
Supplies: You'll need chairs, masking tape, markers, a cassette player, and a musical cassette tape.

This is a winning affirmation game. Before playing, place chairs in a large circle. Be sure there's a chair for each child. Hand each child a strip of masking tape and a marker. Instruct kids to write their names on the tape then stick the tape to the bottoms of their chairs.

Say: **Everyone likes a little pat on the back or a smile to make them feel special. We'll walk in a circle to the music. When the music stops, quickly sit in a chair. When it's your turn, look at the person's name on the tape and say something positive about that person, such as "This person always shares" or "This person is lots of fun to play soccer with." Then we'll guess who you're talking about!**

If the class can't guess in three tries who the person is, have the child who gave the compliment reveal the identity of the person by sticking the masking tape to his or her back.

Turkey Thanks

Best for preschool
Supplies: You'll need poster board, markers, construction paper, tape, scissors, a blindfold, cold turkey sandwich meat, and bread.

Play an exciting game of Pin the Tail on the Turkey with your kids to celebrate all they're thankful for.

Before class, draw a large turkey without tail feathers on a sheet of poster board, then tape the picture to the wall. Cut a colorful turkey feather from construction paper for each child.

Set out markers. Hand kids the paper feathers, then invite kids to draw pictures of things they're thankful for, such as their families, food, or warm clothing. Gather kids around the turkey picture and blindfold one child. Place a small piece of tape on that child's paper feather, then turn him or her around in place a few times. Face the blindfolded child in the direction of the turkey, then tape the feather where he or she thinks it goes. Let the kids read the feathers aloud after everyone has had a turn.

After the game, let kids make their own delicious turkey sandwiches to eat. Be sure to say a prayer of thanksgiving for friends and good food!

Wacky Winter No-Wimpics

Best for early and upper elementary
Supplies: You'll need plastic garbage bags, large marshmallows, and four shoe boxes.

Plan your own Wacky Winter Olympic Games. Set up the following events and let kids "compete" in groups.

● **Sled Races**—Have kids form two lines and race from one end of the room to the other by pushing each other on plastic garbage-bag "sleds."

● **Snowball Tossers**—Have two groups stand on opposing sides of the room. Hand an equal number of large marshmallows to both groups and let them toss the marshmallows at each other. The object of the event is to have no marshmallows on your side of the room after 30 seconds!

● **Swirl 'n' Skate**—Form two lines and take turns "skating" around the room in shoe box "ice skates."

Instead of trophies, consider giving ice-cream cones to all participants.

Working Together

Best for preschool
Supplies: none

Even preschoolers aren't too young to learn about cooperation and teamwork! Before this game, teach children these words to the tune of "Did You Ever See a Lassie?":

When we work together,
Together, together,
When we work together,
We'll find everyone.

Choose one player to be "It." Have It hide his or her eyes while the other children hide. The child who is It looks until he or she finds a friend. The two join hands and sing "When We Work Together." Then both children look for more friends. Each time someone else is found, the friends join hands and sing. Continue playing until all the children are found.

Yarn Circle

Best for preschool
Supplies: You'll need yarn.

Use yarn to make a circle on the floor. Be sure the circle is just large enough for all the kids to stand in. Have kids stand in a circle around the yarn and about four feet away from the circle.

Say: **This circle is for a special person in this room. Let's find out who belongs in this special circle. If you answer "yes" to any question I ask, take a step toward the circle.**

Encourage *all* the children to move forward after each question. Ask:
● **Does God love you?**
● **Is there something special and different about you?**
● **Do you like to laugh and have fun? Do you make mistakes sometimes?**
● **Can you think of something you know how to do, such as jump on one foot across the room?**

By this time, everyone should be inside the circle.

Say: **Look at all the special people we have in our classroom! You're all so special!**

Your Chair, Please

Best for upper elementary
Supplies: You'll need a dice cube and chairs.

This game is designed to encourage kids to put others ahead of themselves.

Before the game, place six chairs in a straight line facing the same direction. If you have more than six kids, make several lines of six chairs facing the same direction. Have each child sit in a chair. Then have kids in each line number off from one to six.

Say: **It's not always easy to put other people before ourselves. In this game, you'll be putting others before you. I'll roll the number cube and tell you the number that comes up. The person sitting in the chair with that number may ask the player in the chair with the next highest number to switch places. Since there's no number seven in our game, the person in the number-six chair can ask to switch places with the person in the number-one chair. That player can decide if he or she wants to switch places. We'll roll the cube ten times and see who's in the number-one chair(s) at the end of the game.**

Roll the die and call out the number rolled. Pause after each roll as kids ask each other to switch places. The faster you roll numbers, the faster the action as kids scramble to get the seat with the lowest number.

After the game, read aloud Philippians 2:3-5 and have kids discuss how it felt for them to put others before themselves. Discuss real-life situations that require them to put others first.

CReaTive Crafts

A Shining Light

Best for upper elementary

Supplies: You'll need nature magazines, a sheet of white paper, 10-inch squares of wax paper, paper lunch sacks, an iron, scissors, sand, tape, and small votive candles.

Preheat the iron at the lowest setting. Be sure to keep the iron away from the kids. Set out paper lunch sacks, nature magazines, 10-inch squares of wax paper, scissors, sand, and the small votive candles. Help kids cut 4-inch circles from one side of their sacks. Then let them browse through magazines and cut out pictures of things (one per person) they're thankful God gave them, such as a family, a house, a special pet, or a favorite food. Tell kids to be sure the picture will fit in the circle on the sack.

Give each child a 10-inch square of wax paper. Have kids lay their pictures on one half of the wax paper then fold the wax paper in half. Help kids lay sheets of white paper over the wax paper, then iron over each child's picture.

Help children tape their waxed pictures to the insides of the sacks, covering the holes. Pour a cup of sand into the bottom of each sack and place a small votive candle in the sand.

Say: **Take this sack home and ask your mother or father to help you light the candle for your dinner table. As you see the light shining through the window, remember that Jesus' light shines through you as you do good things for others.**

Amazing Control

Best for early and upper elementary

Supplies: You'll need box lids, chenille wire, tacky craft glue, and marbles.

Set out chenille wire and tacky craft glue. Give each child a box lid. Be sure the lids have sides. Have kids glue chenille wire to the inside bottom of the lids to form paths for mazes. Remind kids to create some "dead ends."

After the mazes are done, hand each person a marble. Have kids place their marbles in their mazes and tilt the lids back and forth to move their marbles through the mazes. Point out how hard it is to follow the right paths and that it takes a lot of self-control to keep the marbles on track!

Amazing Spinners

Best for preschool and early elementary

Supplies: You'll need poster board, a ruler, a hole punch, scissors, rubber bands, and crayons.

Before this activity, cut a 3-inch poster board circle for each child. Punch a hole on each side of each circle and thread a rubber band through each hole. Pull the rubber bands back through themselves and tighten them until the rubber bands are firmly fastened to the circles.

Set out crayons and the poster board circles. Invite kids to use bright crayons to decorate both sides of their circles. Write "I'm" on one side and "special" on the other side.

Show children how to put their fingers through the rubber bands and wind the rubber bands tight. When children let go, the circles will spin and the words "I'm special" will appear.

Beaded Jewelry

Best for early elementary

Supplies: You'll need toothpicks, shoestrings, and modeling dough (see recipe below).

Before class, make a batch of modeling dough. Use the following recipe: Mix together 1 cup of baking soda, ½ cup of cornstarch, several drops of food coloring, and ¾ cup water. You'll need to mix a batch for each color. Cook over medium heat and stir constantly until the mixture solidifies, but don't overcook it. When the dough cools, knead it until it's smooth and pliable. Store in a tightly covered container.

Have children use this fun dough to create Christmas gifts. Let children make beads of all sizes. Use toothpicks to poke holes through the center of the beads. Be sure the holes are large enough for shoestrings to fit through. Then have children carefully string their beads on the shoestrings.

Let the beads dry for a few days, then color the beads with markers if you desire.

• •

Butterfly and Cross Salt-Dough Ornaments

Best for preschool and early elementary
Supplies: You'll need flour; measuring cups; salt; water; a spoon; food coloring; ribbon; a table; a pencil or toothpick; glitter glue or tempera paints; a cookie sheet; scissors; cookie cutters in a variety of shapes such as butterflies, flowers, animals, and hearts. You'll also need access to an oven.

Before this activity, mix together 2 cups of flour and 2 cups of salt. Gradually add 1 cup of water. Stir until the mixture becomes a ball of dough. If the dough is too sticky, add a bit more flour. Add a few drops of food coloring and knead the dough until it's smooth. You can store salt dough in airtight containers or self-locking plastic bags for a few days.

Hand each child a small lump of salt dough and show kids how to flatten the dough with the palms of their hands. Check to be sure that the children's dough is about ¼ inch thick. Sprinkle a bit of flour on the tabletop, then let each child choose a cookie cutter and cut out a springtime shape. Use a pencil or a toothpick to poke a hole at the top of each dough shape, then lay the shapes on a cookie sheet to air-dry for 48 hours or until they're hard. (You may speed up drying time by "baking" the dough shapes in an oven at 325 degrees for 15 to 20 minutes or until they're hard.)

When the dough shapes are dry, let children embellish them with glitter glue or tempera paints. Thread ribbon through the holes at the top of the "ornaments" so they can hang in windows or on the wall.

T·I·P

Older kids will enjoy embellishing their ornaments with glitter, sequins, buttons, rice, and bits of ribbon. Let their imaginations go wild!

Can-Can Wind Chimes

Best for upper elementary
Supplies: You'll need one large and one small aluminum can for each child. The small can should be small enough to rattle around in the bigger can. You'll also need a Bible, a hammer, masking tape, a table, a nail, newspaper, tempera paint, paintbrushes, and heavy string.

Before class, remove one end from each aluminum can. Wash the cans, then wrap masking tape around the edges to prevent cuts. With a hammer and a nail, punch holes in the center bottom of each can.

Cover a table with newspaper, then set out tempera paint, paintbrushes, and heavy string. Tell kids to paint and decorate the larger can any way they choose, then paint the small cans a solid color. Allow the paint to dry thoroughly.

When the cans are dry, help kids thread string through the holes in the ends of the small cans and tie knots on the inside to prevent the cans from slipping off the strings. Have kids push the other end of each string up through the inside of the larger can and through the hole in its end. Pull the string taut, then tie a loop in the remaining string.

Read aloud Psalm 98:4-9. Ask:
● **Why does the Bible tell us to sing praises to God?**

● **How can you praise God? How can the music of your chimes remind you to praise God this week?**

Let kids take their wind chimes home and hang them outside on patios or trees. Encourage kids to listen to the joyful noises the chimes make to the Lord.

Candy-Cane Candlesticks

Best for upper elementary
Supplies: For each child, you'll need 12 large red and white wrapped candy canes and one 16-inch white candle. You'll also need transparent tape, 1-inch-wide ribbon, bows, and plastic holly or other Christmas decorations.

Give each child 12 large red and white wrapped candy canes and a 16-inch white candle. Have kids find partners to help make their candlesticks, and tell them to make one candlestick at a time.

Have kids tape an upside-down candy cane to each candle. Be sure the candy cane's curve is on the bottom and faces outward. Have kids continue taping candy canes edge to edge so they form a circle around the candle. Make sure the curved ends are even to create a stable base.

Have children run a long piece of transparent tape around the entire candleholder. Have them wrap 1-inch-wide ribbon around the tape to conceal it. Invite each child to attach a bow to the front of his or her candy-cane candlestick. Use plastic holly or other Christmas decorations to make the candlesticks even more festive.

After kids are finished with the candlesticks, ask:

● **How can these candles help people see things more clearly when it's dark?**

● **In John 8:12, Jesus says he is the light of the world. How can Jesus help people who are confused and in the dark?**

● **How can you help someone this week by being a "light" for Jesus?**

Caring for the Sparrow

Best for early elementary

Supplies: You'll need unpeeled oranges (cut into quarters), yarn, a ruler, plastic spoons, peanut butter, scissors, birdseed or popped popcorn, plastic drinking straws, and cornmeal.

This bird-feeder craft teaches young children how great God's love is for them and for his world.

Read aloud Matthew 10:29-31. Then give each child an unpeeled orange quarter. When kids are finished eating their oranges, scrape out any remaining pulp.

Pierce a hole on each side of each orange quarter about midway between the top and the bottom. Insert half of a plastic drinking straw through both holes. Help each child thread a 20-inch piece of yarn through the straw and tie the yarn in a knot. Have children spread peanut butter mixed with cornmeal in their empty quarters and fill them with birdseed or popped popcorn.

Allow children to take their bird feeders home and hang them in trees. Children will see their handiwork being put to use every day as they help God care for the sparrows—and for other birds.

Christmas Blessings Mobile

Best for early and upper elementary

Supplies: You'll need Christmas gift wrap, a ruler, poster board, glue sticks, a stapler, a hole punch, index cards, scissors, markers, and string.

Brighten your classroom with reminders of the things that make Christmas special.

Before class, cut 6×20-inch strips of poster board and Christmas gift wrap. Cut a strip of gift wrap and a strip of poster board for each child.

Set out the poster board and gift wrap strips, glue sticks, stapler, markers, string, scissors, and the hole punch. Have children glue the strips of gift wrap onto the poster board strips. Staple the ends of the poster board strips to make circular rings. Have kids use the hole punch to make six holes around the bottom portion of each ring. Then invite each child to use markers and six index cards to illustrate six things he or she counts as Christmas blessings, such as Jesus, family, friends, or gifts. Then punch holes in the tops of the cards and attach them to the poster board rings with string.

Staple string across the top of each poster board ring, then tie another piece of string to the center to create a hanger. Hang your blessings mobiles from the ceiling and use them to initiate discussions about the true meaning of Christmas and blessings.

Christmas Footprint Cards

Best for early and upper elementary
Supplies: You'll need red and green construction paper, a shallow pan, thin white tempera paint, a table, newspaper, a tub of soapy water, paper towels, and a sponge.

Before this activity, cover a table with newspaper. Set out the tub of soapy water, paper towels, a sponge, and the shallow pan filled with the thin white tempera paint. Hand each child a sheet of red or green construction paper and instruct children to fold their papers in half to make cards. Have the kids take turns dipping the sponge in the paint. Tell them to each make a fist, then have them sponge-paint the sides of their fists. Next have kids press their painted fists on the front of the construction paper cards. Encourage them to roll their fists to leave marks that look like footprints. Then have each child dip one fingertip into the paint and make dots above the "footprint," making what look like toes. Have kids wash their hands in the soapy water.

After the footprints dry, help kids write Isaiah 9:6, "A child has been born to us," on the inside of their cards. Then ask:
● **How can babies be good news for families?**
● **How was baby Jesus good news for the whole world?**
Say: **In Romans 10:15, God says that people who bring good news are beautiful. The good news is that Jesus came to earth. Who are you going to bring good news to with your special Christmas cards?**

Christmas Tree Ornaments

Best for preschool
Supplies: You'll need a photograph of each child or an instant-print camera, old Christmas cards, scissors, glue, red and green markers, clear self-adhesive paper, jars with 2- and 3-inch bases, a ruler, a hole punch, and ribbon.

Preschoolers and their parents will treasure this craft.

Two to three weeks before Christmas, take a photograph of each child in your class and have these pictures developed. Or bring an instant-print camera the day the craft is made.

During craft time, display old Christmas cards and invite each child to choose a card.

Help each child trace a 3-inch circle on his or her Christmas card and a 2-inch circle over his or her photograph. (You can use the base of the jar as a pattern.) Cut out each circle.

Help children glue their photos to the backs of their cards. Use a red or green marker to write the current year below their photos and "Merry Christmas" above. Cover both sides of the ornaments with clear self-adhesive paper. Help kids punch holes through the tops of the ornaments and tie ribbon through the holes for hangers.

Climbing Zacchaeus

Best for preschool and early elementary
Supplies: You'll need a gingerbread-man cookie cutter, poster board, pencils, a ruler, scissors, a hole punch, yarn, crayons, and ½-inch wooden beads.

Before this activity, cut a 6-inch poster board gingerbread man for each child. Use the gingerbread-man cookie cutter as a guide. Punch a hole in each hand and each foot of the paper figures. You'll also need to cut a 6-foot piece of yarn for each child.

Set out crayons and hand each child a paper figure of Zacchaeus. Let kids decorate their paper figures. Then help each child thread a 6-foot piece of yarn through the right foot and the right hand, loop it over the

head, and thread it through the left hand and the left foot. Tie a ½-inch wooden bead to each end of the yarn. Have children take turns looping their yarn over a doorknob. As children gently pull the yarn out to the sides, Zacchaeus will "climb" up the yarn!

Creation Collages

Best for preschool
Supplies: You'll need poster board; a ruler; 3-inch-wide masking tape; a cookie sheet; and natural objects such as leaves, grass, small flowers or flower petals, and sand.

Toddlers enjoy tactile activities, and this craft will give them lots to touch and explore!

Before this activity, cut 5×12-inch poster board strips. You'll need one strip for each child.

Set out grass, small flowers or flower petals, leaves, and sand in a cookie sheet. Cut a 10-inch section of 3-inch-wide masking tape for each child. Lay each piece of tape on a poster board strip with the sticky side of the tape facing up. Slightly bend the ends of the tape under to secure them to the poster board.

Invite children to stick flowers, leaves, grass, and sand to the tape to create a "sticky collage." As children work, talk about the many wonderful things God made in the world around us.

Eggshell Mosaics

Best for preschool
Supplies: You'll need construction paper, a table, newspaper, white craft glue, markers, paintbrushes, and colored eggshells from Easter eggs.

This craft is lots of fun and is a creative way to use the colored eggshells from your Easter eggs. Before this activity, gently break the eggshells into small pieces. You may even wish to have kids contribute eggshells from their Easter eggs! You'll also need to draw large, simple outlines on construction paper, such as Easter crosses, Humpty Dumpty figures, or flowers. Draw an outline for each child.

Cover a table with newspaper. Place the eggshells in easy-to-reach piles on the table. Set out white craft glue and paintbrushes. Make sure you have a paintbrush for each child. Distribute the outlines and show kids how to brush glue over a small portion of each picture then stick eggshells to the glue. When the outlines have been filled in with eggshell bits, set the pictures aside to dry.

T·I·P

Preschoolers will enjoy acting out the nursery rhyme "Humpty Dumpty" as they wait for their pictures to dry.

Empty Tombs

Best for early elementary
Supplies: You'll need brown construction paper, white paper, crayons, pencils, and paper fasteners.

Let kids create a tactile picture of the first Easter morning. Set out brown construction paper, crayons, pencils, and paper fasteners. Hand each child a sheet of white paper and invite each student to draw hillsides with a cave opening in one of the hills. Help kids write in the open space of the caves, " 'He is not here. He has risen.' Matthew 28:6." Then have children tear out brown construction paper "stones" to cover the cave openings. Help kids attach the paper stones to the caves with paper fasteners so the stones can be "rolled away" to reveal the verse.

Lead children in repeating the verse several times. Encourage the children to take their pictures home and read the verse to their families.

Face Painting

Best for all ages
Supplies: You'll need paint shirts; paintbrushes; and red, white, and blue face paint.

Set your kids "free" with this fun Independence Day activity!

Have kids don paint shirts and get with partners. Using red, white, and blue face paint, have kids paint stars and stripes on each other's faces. Have them use a separate paintbrush for each color. You might suggest that they paint other shapes, including flags, fireworks, and smiley faces.

Tell children to keep their hands away from their painted faces until the paint is dry.

If you'd rather make your own face paints, try this recipe:
● 1 cup solid vegetable shortening
● 1 cup cornstarch
● food coloring

Mix shortening and cornstarch until there are no lumps. If the mixture is too thick, add a few drops of water; if it's too thin, add ¼ teaspoon of shortening. Divide the mixture into three bowls. Use food coloring to make a bowl of red paint and a bowl of blue paint. The remaining bowl is white paint.

Face paints can be refrigerated in sealed plastic containers for up to three days.

Gift Cartons

Best for early elementary

Supplies: You'll need empty pint milk cartons, felt, scissors, tacky craft glue, greeting cards, glitter glue, shredded paper or Easter grass, and a variety of individually wrapped candies.

Before this activity, cut the tops off empty pint milk cartons. Rinse out the cartons and allow them to dry.

Set out the craft materials and help each child cut a piece of felt large enough to wrap around a carton. Have kids glue the felt to the milk cartons. Let children cut pictures from greeting cards then glue the pictures to the felt. Have kids embellish the pictures with glitter glue. Children can place shredded paper or Easter grass in the cartons then add individually wrapped candies to the cartons and give them as special gifts.

Glue-and-Glitter Butterflies

Best for early and upper elementary

Supplies: You'll need a Bible, wax paper, glitter, sheets of paper, markers, tape, a cookie sheet, fishing line, and glue.

Set out the glue, glitter, markers, cookie sheet, and tape. Hand each child a sheet of paper on which to draw the outline of a medium-sized butterfly. Hand children sheets of wax paper and tape the wax paper to their butterfly outlines. Let kids use streams of glue to trace the outlines of their butterflies. Then have each child

carefully set his or her picture on the cookie sheet and sprinkle glitter over the wet glue. Carefully set the papers aside to dry for a few days.

When the butterflies are completely dry, carefully peel them from the wax paper. Thread a length of fishing line through each butterfly. Hang the butterflies from the ceiling or in a window where they can sparkle and blow in the breeze!

Read aloud 2 Corinthians 5:17. Ask:
● **How is a butterfly like a new creation?**
● **What makes us become new creations in Christ?**
● **What's one thing about you that shows that you're a new creation in Christ?**

Close in prayer, thanking God for our new life through Jesus' death and resurrection.

Hand-Print Apron Gift

Best for preschool to upper elementary
Supplies: You'll need scissors, muslin, a sewing machine, bias tape, acrylic fabric paint, paintbrushes, newspaper, and permanent markers.

With a touch of the sewing needle, you'll have these aprons ready in a jiffy! Cut an adult-size bib-apron shape from muslin. Hem the edges. Sew a continuous piece of bias tape along the top edges to form the neck strap and the ties around the waist. If sewing gets you "in a stitch," you can purchase inexpensive ready-made aprons at most craft stores.

Cover your work area with newspaper. Let kids brush acrylic fabric paint on their hands then make hand prints on the aprons. Older kids may wish to use paintbrushes to paint designs or words. Encourage kids to use a rainbow of colors. Be sure to have kids sign their names with paint somewhere on their aprons. Help young children print their names with permanent markers.

Have children present their aprons to their moms or dads for Mother's Day or Father's Day.

Heart Watchers

Best for preschool and early elementary
Supplies: You'll need red or pink construction paper, two wiggly craft eyes for each child, tape, glue, and an unsharpened pencil for each child.

Use these cute heart crafts to decorate your houseplants and to give them a "little love."

Before class, cut a variety of hearts from red or pink construction paper. Be sure there's a paper heart for each child.

Set out tape, unsharpened pencils, paper hearts, glue, and the wiggly craft eyes. If you have children under 6 years of age, substitute cereal loops for the wiggly eyes to avoid a swallowing hazard.

Let each child choose a paper heart then glue wiggly eyes to one side of the heart. Have the child tape the eraser-end of a pencil flat against the other side of the paper heart. Encourage children to give their Heart Watchers to their parents, who may stick them in houseplants as pretty decorations!

I Want to Praise Jesus!

Best for preschool
Supplies: You'll need one empty frozen-juice can (keep the pull-off lid) for each child, jingle bells, small rocks, aluminum foil, and duct tape.

Before this activity, collect empty frozen-juice cans with the pull-off lids. You'll need the lids for this craft idea, too. Be sure to have one can and one lid for each child.

Hand each child a juice can. Let children place a few small rocks and a jingle bell in each can. Help children attach the lids to the cans and wrap duct tape around the lids to secure them to the cans. Have children wrap their "musical praise instruments" with aluminum foil.

When everyone's musical instrument is finished, form a "praise band" and sing the following song as kids shake their instruments in time to the music (to the tune of "Row, Row, Row Your Boat"):

Sing, sing, sing for joy!
Jesus is alive.
I am happy, I am happy—
Jesus is alive!

Substitute other action words in place of "sing," such as "clap," "jump," "whisper," or "shout."

— T·I·P —

These cute pretzel goodies are nice gifts for kids to make. Simply let kids decorate small boxes, then fill the boxes with these sweet treats and give them as special gifts of love.

In My Heart

Best for early and upper elementary
Supplies: You'll need large three-ring pretzels and large marshmallows.

Hand each child two large three-ring pretzels and two large marshmallows. Show kids how to gently nibble the center from their pretzels to create open spaces. Point out that the open spaces look like empty hearts. Hold up the marshmallows and mention that we can fill empty hearts with something sweet. Show kids how to push the marshmallows into the open spaces where they'll stick in place.

When everyone has the two hearts "filled," let kids nibble on the treats, and talk about Jesus as the only one who fills our hearts!

Lambs of God

Best for nursery and preschool
Supplies: You'll need a Bible, cotton balls, a glue stick, craft sticks, tape, poster board, and scissors.

For each child, cut a lamb-shaped mask from poster board. Cut a hole—big enough for the child's face—in the center of the mask.

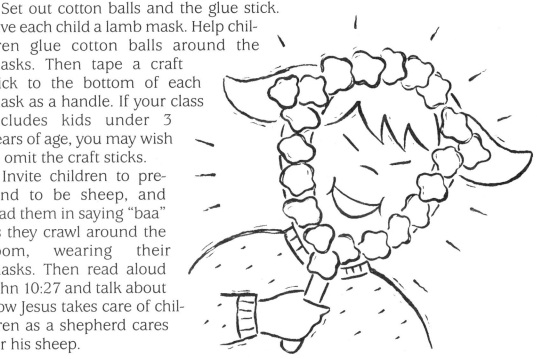

Set out cotton balls and the glue stick. Give each child a lamb mask. Help children glue cotton balls around the masks. Then tape a craft stick to the bottom of each mask as a handle. If your class includes kids under 3 years of age, you may wish to omit the craft sticks.

Invite children to pretend to be sheep, and lead them in saying "baa" as they crawl around the room, wearing their masks. Then read aloud John 10:27 and talk about how Jesus takes care of children as a shepherd cares for his sheep.

Leafy T-Shirts

Best for upper elementary
Supplies: You'll need a Bible, newspaper, a heavy book, fabric paint, paintbrushes, water, a table, small craft sponges, fresh green leaves, and solid-colored T-shirts.

A week before making this craft, press fresh green leaves in a heavy book between layers of newspaper. Press until the leaves are flat. You'll want a few leaves for each color of fabric paint you're planning to use. Arrange for kids to bring their own solid-colored T-shirts to decorate, or purchase an inexpensive T-shirt for each child.

Cover a table with newspaper. Show children how to fold newspaper then slide the newspaper inside their T-shirts so the fabric paint won't bleed through the T-shirts. Be sure the newspaper lies flat. Instruct kids to lay their shirts on the table and to smooth out wrinkles in the fabric.

With a damp paintbrush, lightly coat a small craft sponge with fabric paint. Show the kids how to dab the sponge on the veined side of a leaf, including the stem. Make sure they understand that they should *press* the

T·I·P

It's important to show the children each step of this craft before they do it on their own. Use a paper grocery sack as a sample "shirt."

sponge on the leaf rather than rub it. Gently press the leaf on a T-shirt, paint side down. Carefully pick up the leaf. Adjust the amount of paint on the next leaf as necessary. Leave the newspaper inside the T-shirts until the paint is dry.

As you're waiting for the paint to dry, read Revelation 4:11 aloud and discuss God's wonderful gift of creation. Encourage kids to tell about their favorite parts of creation, such as leaves, special animals, clouds, or people.

Love Cookies

Best for upper elementary
Supplies: You'll need a pan of unsliced, baked cookie bars or brownies; wire cutters; 20-gauge green floral wire; scissors; a ruler; red satin ribbon; plastic sandwich bags; a heart-shaped cookie cutter; and a spatula.

Be sure the cookie bars or brownies are already prepared. Then cut 18-inch lengths of the green floral wire. Cut one wire "stem" for each child. Cut the red satin ribbon into a 9-inch piece for each child.

Set out the heart-shaped cookie cutter, the plastic sandwich bags, the pieces of floral wire, and the lengths of ribbon. Let the kids take turns using the cookie cutter to cut out heart-shaped cookies. Push hard so the cookie cutter goes to the bottom of the pan on all sides. Slip each cookie into a plastic sandwich bag. Fold each piece of wire in half, then insert the pointed ends into the bottom edge of a cookie so the heart will be right-side-up when it's held by the wires. Tie a red ribbon bow around the base of each cookie to seal the bag closed.

Say: **In John 15:17, Jesus spoke to the disciples, saying, "This is my command: Love each other." Is it always easy to love each other? Why or why not? Let's thank God for the family and friends he's given us to love.** Have children give the cookies to people they love.

Love Loops

Best for early elementary
Supplies: You'll need red yarn, a ruler, scissors, and a box of fruit-flavored cereal loops.

Give your children a new way to praise God and to show their love for him.

Have kids form a circle. Give each child a 36-inch piece of red yarn and 10 fruit-flavored cereal loops. Have children tell reasons they love God. Whenever a child gives an answer, have <u>everyone</u> string a cereal loop on his or her yarn piece then tie the loop in place with a knot. Challenge the kids to name so many reasons that they'll make complete necklaces!

Once kids are finished with their praises, have them tie their Love

Loops loosely around their necks to wear as necklaces—reminders of how much they love God and how much God loves them.

Made by Everybunny

Best for early and upper elementary
Supplies: You'll need 6×6-inch fabric scraps, rubber bands, scissors, ribbon, a ruler, tacky craft glue, wiggly craft eyes, ½-inch black pompons, and cotton balls.

Before this activity, cut 12-inch lengths of ribbon. Cut one piece of ribbon for each child.

Read aloud Ecclesiastes 4:9. Then say: **Let's work together to make something special for each of us. This project will help us see how important it is to cooperate and to help each other.**

Form the following six-station assembly line with children divided evenly among the stations: station 1—roll up a 6×6-inch fabric scrap; station 2—secure a rubber band at the "neck" of the fabric scrap; station 3—tie a 12-inch ribbon over the rubber band; station 4—glue wiggly craft eyes just below the ribbon; station 5—glue a ½-inch black pompon "nose" below the eyes; station 6—glue a cotton ball to the back of the "bunny." Have kids assemble enough bunnies for everyone in the room.

Afterward, tie a bunny to each child's wrist, using extra ribbon. Say: **You worked together to make these bunnies, and they'll help you remember that each of you is "somebunny" special!**

Moses in the Bulrushes

Best for preschool

Supplies: You'll need white paper plates, blue plastic wrap, cotton balls, birdseed, glue sticks, water, unshelled peanuts, scissors, halved walnut shells, and fabric scraps.

Use this craft to teach the story of Moses as a baby. Emphasize that God took special care of Moses in spite of the fact that Moses faced many evils, even as a baby.

Have children tightly cover their white paper plates with blue plastic wrap. Then have each child glue cotton balls on about one-third of his or her plate. Have kids group the cotton balls together for a more striking effect. Dampen the cotton balls, then help children sprinkle birdseed on the cotton.

Let children draw faces on their unshelled peanuts. Help children cut fabric scraps and glue the scraps—swaddling clothes—on their figures of "baby Moses." Have kids place their babies in walnut-shell halves and place the "baskets" on the blue plastic wrap "water."

Tell children to care for the cotton balls at home by keeping them moistened with water, just as God took care of Moses. Within a day or two, the birdseed will sprout. By the end of the week, the child will have a gorgeous depiction of baby Moses among the bulrushes!

My Manger

Best for preschool

Supplies: You'll need letter-size envelopes, scissors, modeling dough, crayons, tape, and Easter grass or shredded wheat biscuits.

Before this activity, cut the flaps off letter-size envelopes. Prepare an envelope for each child.

Give each child an envelope with the flap cut off and a small lump of modeling dough. Help children form babies from their modeling dough. Invite children to decorate their envelopes, using crayons. Fold and tape each lower envelope corner so it lies flat on the bottom fold of the envelope (see illustration). This will enable the envelope to stand up as a "manger." Give each child a handful of Easter grass or a shredded wheat biscuit to break up into the manger as pretend straw. Have children place the modeling dough "babies" on top of the straw.

Close your craft time by singing "Away in a Manger."

• •

Name Game Headbands

Best for preschool
Supplies: You'll need brown paper grocery sacks, tape, markers, scissors, a ruler, and colorful stickers.

Before this activity, cut a brown paper grocery sack into a 2×24-inch strip for each child.

Set out markers, colorful stickers, and the paper strips. Invite each child to decorate a paper strip, then write each child's name on his or her paper. Help kids make headbands from the paper strips by wrapping the paper bands around their heads then taping the ends of each strip together.

Let kids show each other their handiwork, then play a name game using the headbands. Sit in a circle, then invite children to take turns pointing to their headbands and saying their names aloud. Choose a child to stand in the center of the circle. Have someone raise his or her hand and have the child standing in the center try to guess the name of that child. Then let those two kids switch places. Play until everyone has had a chance to stand in the center of the circle and say a name.

T·I·P

Headbands are a great twist on traditional name tags—and kids love wearing headbands!

Napkin Rings

Best for early elementary
Supplies: You'll need cardboard tubes, a ruler, markers, sequins, ribbon bits, scissors, tacky craft glue, and paper towels.

Cut cardboard tubes into 2-inch segments or rings. Cut enough rings that you have one for each member of every child's family.

Set out ribbon bits, sequins, markers, and the tacky craft glue. Hand each child the number of rings he or she needs. Invite everyone to decorate a napkin ring for each member of his or her family. Then let kids roll up paper towels and insert these "napkins" through the napkin rings.

Say: **Give these napkin rings to your family as a gift of love. As you eat, remember to practice good manners and to thank God for your family.**

Party Hats

Best for preschool
Supplies: You'll need plastic-foam plates and bowls, masking tape, tissue paper squares, ribbons, markers, and glue.

Preschoolers love hats! Here's an easy way for them to make their own!
Cut the center out of plastic-foam plates. Push plastic-foam bowls up through the holes in the plates, with the bottom of the bowls pointing up

to create bowler-style hats. Tape the bowls in place with masking tape. Invite children to decorate their new "hats" with tissue paper squares, markers, and ribbons.

Pleasin' Popcorn Hearts

Best for early and upper elementary
Supplies: You'll need a Bible, wire cutters, plastic-foam packaging "popcorn," curling ribbon, thin wire, and scissors.

Before this activity, cut thin wire into 18-inch pieces. Cut one piece of wire for each child.

Set out the wire, plastic-foam packaging "popcorn," curling ribbon, and scissors. Have kids string the foam popcorn pieces onto pieces of wire. Tell kids to be sure to leave about one inch of space at the ends of their wires. Have them twist the two ends of each wire together then bend the circles of popcorn pieces into heart shapes. They can add curled pieces of ribbon to the top of the hearts to decorate them.

When everyone's finished, have children look at the hearts. Read aloud Ephesians 4:32. Ask:

- **Are these hearts strong or fragile? Explain.**
- **What happens when we're mean to others or we hurt their feelings?**
- **How can we treat others as though their hearts are fragile?**

Prayer Tree

Best for early and upper elementary
Supplies: You'll need small fallen branches, plastic or paper cups, modeling dough or florists clay, tape, small slips of paper, pencils, a ruler, and ribbons.

Take a springtime walk with your kids and have them watch out for and collect small fallen branches. When you return, have kids "plant" the branches in plastic or paper cups by sticking modeling dough or florists clay in the bottom of the cups then poking the branches into the dough or clay. Encourage kids to write or draw prayer requests on small slips of paper then tape the slips of paper to the branches. Challenge kids to take their prayer trees home and to pray about their concerns. Give each child a foot of ribbon to take home. When a prayer is answered, the child can remove the slip of paper representing that request and tie a ribbon bow in it's place.

Pretty Medallion Necklaces

Best for early elementary

Supplies: You'll need yarn, a ruler, scissors, stickers, tape, and aluminum can lids from frozen-juice cans that don't require a can opener.

Before this activity, collect an aluminum can lid for each child. Be sure these lids come from frozen-juice cans that have "zip strips" and that can be opened without a can opener. Be sure there are no sharp edges on the lids. Also, cut a 24-inch piece of yarn for each child.

Set out stickers, yarn pieces, and tape. Distribute the juice-can lids and let each child choose a sticker to place on the front of his or her lid. Help each child attach both ends of a piece of yarn to his or her lid to make a shiny medallion to wear.

Pretty, Perky Plants

Best for preschool and early elementary

Supplies: You'll need paper plates, markers, tape, a hole punch, cupcake papers, tissue paper, crepe paper, a stapler, scissors, a ruler, and ribbon.

Before this activity, cut ribbon into 6-inch lengths. You'll need to cut four pieces of ribbon for each child.

Set out markers, tape, cupcake papers, tissue paper, crepe paper, and the hole punch. Hand each child four paper plates and invite kids to use the markers, crepe paper, tissue paper, and cupcake papers to make a flower in the center of each paper plate. Encourage kids to be creative and to use bright colors such as red, yellow, and green.

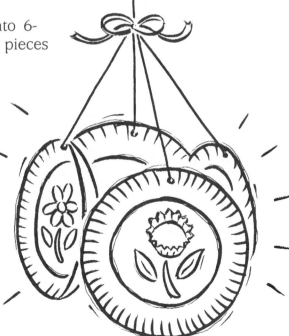

After the children finish, staple the plates edge to edge so each plate forms a side of a square, with the artwork on the outside. Let kids punch holes in the top of the paper plates. Thread ribbon through each hole and tie the ribbons to the paper plates. Tie the four pieces of ribbon together at the ends, and hang the plates as a mobile.

Pretzel Wreaths

Best for early and upper elementary
Supplies: You'll need small pretzels, small round cinnamon candies, curling ribbon, scissors, a ruler, and tacky craft glue or a hot-glue gun. (Children should be carefully supervised with a hot-glue gun. You can use tacky glue, but a hot-glue gun is much faster.)

Before this activity, cut curling ribbon into 10-inch lengths. Cut a piece of ribbon for each child.

Set out the craft items and show kids how to form a circle of six small pretzels with the pretzel edges touching and the indented side facing out. Help children use tacky craft glue to glue the edges of their pretzels together to form a wreath shape. Add another circle of pretzels to the first circle, gluing the second layer to the underside of the first. If you're using a hot-glue gun, do this portion of the craft for the children then set the glue gun out of reach.

Show kids how to weave curling ribbon through the pretzels on their wreaths. Be sure to leave two inches of ribbon at each end, then tie the ends together. Tie extra ribbon on the wreaths as hangers, then let kids glue small round cinnamon candies on the pretzel wreaths.

Say: **God's love is like a never-ending circle. John 3:16 says God loves us so much that he sent Jesus to earth for us.** Ask:
● **What did Jesus do for us that showed God's love?**
● **What is another way God has shown his love for you?**
● **How can you show God's love to someone else?**

Re-creating

Best for early elementary
Supplies: You'll need index cards, markers, and crayons.

Hand each child seven index cards. Set out markers and crayons. Invite kids to draw simple symbols for the days of Creation, such as black and white halves of a card (day 1—day and night), water (day 2—air and water), mountains and an apple tree (day 3—land and plants), stars and a moon or sun (day 4—heavenly bodies), birds and fish (day 5), animals and a person (day 6), and the word "rest" (day 7—God rested).

Then have children shuffle their picture cards. On "go," have children race to rearrange the picture squares with the seven days of Creation in order. Let kids trade cards with friends and put their friends' picture squares in order.

Recycled Sewing Cards

Best for preschool
Supplies: You'll need empty cereal boxes, scissors, crayons, markers, coloring book pictures, a yard stick, a hole punch, yarn, and cellophane tape.

Ahead of time, open and flatten empty cereal boxes to use as backing for sewing cards. Glue coloring book pictures on the pieces of cardboard from the cereal boxes. Pictures from Bible coloring books work especially well. Punch holes about two inches apart around the edges of the pictures to create sewing cards. You'll also need to cut a yard of yarn for each child.

Set out the sewing cards, crayons and markers, and yarn. Invite each child to choose a picture to color. Then hand each child a piece of yarn. Help kids tie a knot at one end of each piece of yarn then wrap a bit of cellophane tape around the other end of the yarn. This will make it easier to pass the yarn through the holes on the sewing cards. Show kids how to "sew" the edges of their cards in running stitches or loops.

Scripture-Advent Chain

Best for early and upper elementary
Supplies: You'll need a Bible; a sheet of paper; scissors; a marker; tape; red, green, and white construction paper; and access to a photocopy machine.

Before this activity, make a list of 25 favorite Bible verses or divide the story of Jesus' birth in the Gospel of Luke into verses and write them on a sheet of paper. Space the verses one inch apart. If you choose to use the story of Jesus' birth, number the verses in sequential order. Photocopy the list of verses onto red, green, and white construction paper, then cut apart the verses to make paper strips.

Set out the construction paper strips and tape. Let kids make paper chains by linking the paper strips together and taping the ends. Be sure kids use all 25 verses. If you're using the story of Jesus' birth, make sure the verses are in sequential order from left to right.

Tell kids to hang their chains up at home and, beginning December first, to tear off a link and read the verse each day. They will read the last verse on Christmas Day!

Seasonal Paper Plate Wreaths

Best for early elementary
Supplies: You'll need a Bible, scissors, gift wrap, white craft glue, a hole punch, ribbon, poster board or old file folders, and paper plates.

Celebrate the seasons with these wild wreaths! Before starting, cut seasonal patterns from poster board or old file folders. Here are suggestions for patterns to make for each month or season: January—snowflakes; February—heart shapes; March and April—flowers, bunnies, crosses, or eggs; September, October, and November—leaves or pumpkins; December—stars or angels.

Set out paper plates, scissors, white craft glue, gift wrap, and the seasonal patterns you've chosen. Instruct kids to cut the center from their paper plates. Show kids how to fold gift wrap (or construction paper) into fourths. Then let kids trace the seasonal patterns onto the folded paper and cut out several shapes at once. Have children glue the shapes around the edges of the paper plates.

Have kids punch holes at the top of their wreaths then thread ribbon through the holes and make loops for hanging the wreaths.

When you're finished, read Ecclesiastes 3:1. Ask:
- **Why do we celebrate this season?**
- **What can we enjoy and thank God for at this time of year?**

Special, Special People!

Best for upper elementary
Supplies: You'll need prepared cookie dough; cookie sheets; a variety of craft materials such as poster board, ribbon, glue, sequins, tissue paper, and buttons; and access to an oven.

Distribute prepared cookie dough to children and invite them to create special "people" with the dough. Carefully place the cookie people on cookie sheets and ask an adult volunteer to take the cookies to the kitchen and bake them.

While the cookies are baking, have children form groups of three. Give each group a variety of craft materials. Have group members nominate each other to represent different body parts; for example, they may say, "You're the hands because you're helpful" or "You're the eyes because you see people's needs." Have kids use the craft materials to make awards for their group members. When the cookies are done, celebrate the "body of Christ" by enjoying the cookie treats and giving out the awards the children have made. Be sure everyone is affirmed with an award.

Spiritual Sandals

Best for upper elementary

Supplies: You'll need brown poster board, pencils, scissors, a ruler, a hole punch, and yarn.

Before class, cut two 20-inch pieces of yarn for each child.

Lay several sheets of brown poster board on the floor. Have kids stand on the poster board and trace their feet. Let kids cut out the outlines then write or draw on them things that may be detours, distractions, or dangers on the road of life, such as lying or disobeying God.

Then help kids punch holes one inch apart along the edges of each foot. Give each child two 20-inch lengths of yarn. Have kids tie a knot at one end of each piece of yarn and lace it through the holes. Have them repeat this process for the other paper foot.

After kids are finished with their sandals, have them tie their lengths of yarn together. Encourage kids to hang their sandals in their rooms to remind themselves that Jesus is their guide.

Spray Art

Best for preschool and early elementary

Supplies: You'll need used spray bottles, ammonia, water, food coloring, masking tape, a 20-foot piece of rope, clothespins, sheets of newsprint, and paint shirts.

Before class, ask people to donate used spray bottles, such as hair spray or cleaner bottles. Wash and rinse all the bottles and pumps thoroughly. Then fill each spray bottle with colored water. Label the bottles with masking tape.

Tie a 20-foot piece of rope between two trees or poles outside, about three feet above the ground. Attach sheets of newsprint to the rope with clothespins.

Have each child wear a paint shirt and stand by a sheet of newsprint. Let kids "paint" pictures, using the spray bottles of colored water. The colors will mix, creating beautiful paintings. Once a child is finished with his or her painting, remove it and allow it to dry on the grass.

Spring Praise to God

Best for early elementary

Supplies: You'll need neon paper, scissors, a ruler, and tape.

Before this activity, cut ½×12-inch strips of neon paper. Cut at least four strips for each child.

Hand each child two ½×12-inch strips of neon paper. Help children make praise springs: Lay the end of one strip over the end of the other strip to make an L shape. Alternate folding the first strip on top of the second and the second strip on top of the first until the strips are completely folded into one square. Tape each end of the square to make a spring. Let each child make two neon springs.

Have children lay their springs in their hands. When you say, "Praise God," have each child push down on one of his or her springs then let it spring up. Then when you say, "Praise him all the time," have each child push down on the other spring and let it go.

Super Scribble Box

Best for nursery and preschool
Supplies: You'll need crayons, a large appliance box, butcher paper, and tape.

One- and 2-year-olds love coloring on anything! Instead of snatching away crayons as toddlers head for walls, designate a "scribble area." Line the inside of a large appliance box, including the bottom, with butcher paper. Then cover the outside of the box with butcher paper. Place a few crayons in the box and limit the number of children who are allowed inside the box to color at one time. Encourage toddlers to take turns coloring in and on the box. Replace the butcher paper when it's reached its "artistic limit!"

T·I·P

For a colorful twist, cover the box with pastel-colored paper or paper with a large checked pattern. Your little ones will think they have an exciting new "coloring book!"

Valentine Cards

Best for early and upper elementary
Supplies: You'll need 10×10-inch sheets of poster board, heart-shaped sponges, aluminum pie pans, tempera paint, pencils, scissors, glitter glue, sequins, markers, colored construction paper, magazines, and glue.

Make cheery Valentine cards, then give them to people you love.
   Have kids follow these directions to make their special cards:
   1. Fold 10×10-inch sheets of poster board in half to make cards. Pour one color of tempera paint into each aluminum pie pan. Dip the heart-shaped sponges in tempera paint. Gently press the sponges on the cards

to make prints. Allow the paint to dry.

2. Trace one hand on a sheet of poster board, then cut out the paper hand print. Decorate the paper hand print, using glitter glue, sequins, and markers. Write on each hand print sayings such as "I'll *hand* it to you—you're lovable" or "I love you, so give yourself a pat on the back!"

3. Cut out hearts from colored construction paper or colorful magazine ads. Glue the hearts to the front of the cards to make colorful collages.

4. Encourage kids to tell who they'll give their special cards to.

Weaving in the Round

Best for early elementary
Supplies: You'll need a Bible; scissors; a ruler; thick yarn; card stock paper; strips of fabric, ribbon, and braid; and plastic lids from coffee or soft drink mix cans.

Before this activity, cut rows of ½-inch-wide slits all across each plastic lid. Prepare a lid for each child in class. You'll also need to cut ½×10-inch lengths of ribbon, fabric, braid, thick yarn, and card stock paper for kids to weave with. Be sure to provide a variety of textures and colors for kids to use.

Set out the weaving strips and hand each child a plastic lid. Show kids how to weave strips of paper and fabric through the slits on the plastic lids. Encourage kids to use lots of colors and patterns.

When children are finished, invite them to hold up their handiwork and tell about what they've made. Then read Exodus 35:35 aloud. Say: **God gave the people great weaving skills. God gives everyone different skills. What do you like to do?** Have kids mention several things they're good at or enjoy doing. **Let's remember to thank God for giving us so many wonderful skills.**

Y'all Come Back

Best for early and upper elementary
Supplies: You'll need poster board; scissors; a fine-tip marker; ribbons; sequins; pin backings; glue; and pictures from magazines, greeting cards, or gift wrap.

Kids can learn that it's important to encourage one another to attend church.

Have kids cut pictures from greeting cards, magazines, or gift wrap. Have kids cut out poster board shapes then glue the pictures to the shapes. Let kids embellish their pictures with sequins and ribbons. Then help them glue pin backings to the backs of the poster board shapes.

When the pins are finished and drying, ask:

● **Why is it important to God that we come to church?**

● **What are ways we can encourage our friends to come to church?**

Encourage kids to give their pins to friends as invitations to come to church with them next week.

Year-Round Tree

Best for all ages

Supplies: You'll need cardboard tubes; blue paper; markers; a bulletin board or a bare wall; brown tempera paint; pins, craft glue, or duct tape; cotton balls; paper doilies; paintbrushes; a pencil; a camera; tape; scissors; a white sheet of paper; construction paper; popped popcorn; and access to a photocopy machine.

Let kids help make a neat bulletin board that lasts all year. Collect cardboard tubes and cut them in half.

Put a blue paper background on a bulletin board or a bare wall. Use markers to draw the outline of a tree trunk. Paint the tube halves with brown tempera paint. Then use pins, craft glue, or duct tape to attach the tubes to the bulletin board tree as branches.

Let kids help decorate their classroom "tree" for each season.

● **Summer**—Have kids tear large green construction paper leaves to put on the tree. Then take a photograph of each child and tape each picture to a leaf. When summer is over, give the leaves and the pictures to children to take home with them.

● **Fall**—Draw leaf shapes on a white sheet of paper, then photocopy the leaf shapes onto sheets of construction paper in autumn colors such as brown, yellow, and orange. Cut out the shapes. Help children write or draw on the leaves pictures of things they're thankful for. Tape the leaves to the bulletin board tree. Around Thanksgiving, let the leaves "fall" from your tree by taking down the paper leaves and letting kids take them home.

● **Winter**—Let kids tape stretched-out cotton balls along the branches of the tree to represent shivery snow. Hang paper doilies around the tree as snowflakes.

● **Spring**—Let the "snow" on your tree melt away, and add popped-popcorn "blossoms" to the branches. Create construction paper tulips and tape them along the bottom of the bulletin board. Help kids write or draw on the tulips ways they've grown this year.

Seasonal Ideas

Amazing Bean Scene *(Spring)*

Best for preschool and early elementary
Supplies: You'll need a Bible, colorful markers, wet paper towels, mung beans, plastic wrap, rubber bands, a pencil, and plastic-foam cups.

Set out plastic-foam cups, markers, mung beans, plastic wrap, rubber bands, and wet paper towels. Gather kids, then read aloud Matthew 19:26. Say: **God does things every day that seem impossible. We don't know how some of these things happen, but we believe that God will continue his miracles. This week you'll have a chance to watch your own miracle happen. We're going to plant seeds without using dirt, and by next week God will help them grow.**

Invite each child to use colorful markers to decorate a cup. Demonstrate how to put wet paper towels in the bottom of the cups then to sprinkle a few beans on the paper towels. Have kids cover their cups with plastic wrap then secure the plastic with rubber bands. Help kids use a pencil to carefully punch small air holes in the plastic wrap.

Say: **Growing seeds are like tiny miracles from God. What starts out dried and looking dead becomes green and alive. Keep the paper towels in your cup damp and set the cup in a sunny window. Before long you'll see a miracle of growth that will remind you of God's miracles.**

Are You a Puppet? *(Back to School)*

Best for preschool and early elementary
Supplies: You'll need paper lunch sacks, tape, construction paper, yarn bits, and crayons.

Set out paper lunch sacks, yarn bits, tape, construction paper, and crayons. As children arrive, invite them to create puppet people from the lunch sacks and other craft supplies.

When everyone's puppet is finished, say: **Sometimes it's hard to make good choices of what to do or say. We can use our puppet friends to act out good choices.**

Read the following situations one at a time. After each situation, let willing children use their puppets to act out a good choice for that situation.

● **You're playing at a friend's house, and your friend tells you to steal some cookies from the cookie jar. What will you do?**

● **Your parents tell you not to watch television, but when they go outside, your sister tells you to turn it on anyway. What will you do?**

● **Your teacher says not to run in the hallway, but all your friends run anyway. What can you do?**

Say: **Sometimes we do things that other people do. Sometimes we act or talk before thinking. It's important to make good choices and to not just follow other people if what they're doing is wrong. Jesus wants us to think like people—not like puppets.**

Be Kind to Butterflies (Spring)

Best for early elementary
Supplies: You'll need paper, clothespins, tacky craft glue, scissors, a ruler, 4×6-inch squares of tissue paper, sequins, glitter glue, and markers.

Before this activity, draw a simple picture of a wiggly caterpillar. You'll also need to cut tissue paper into 4×6-inch squares.

Have kids form two groups: the "badgers" and the "bunnies." Tell kids the badgers are mean and like to make fun of others but the bunnies are kind and helpful.

Show kids the picture of the caterpillar as you tell a short story about a caterpillar who wanted to fly but couldn't. End your story with the caterpillar trying to fly but falling instead. Have the badgers and the bunnies role play their responses to the fallen caterpillar. For example, the badgers might laugh and say, "Silly caterpillar—you'll never fly!" And the bunnies might respond with "Poor caterpillar. I'll help you."

After the story, ask:
● How did the caterpillar feel when it couldn't fly?
● Which group made Jesus sad by the way it treated the caterpillar? Why?
● Which group made Jesus happy? Why?

Say: **There are times when each of us needs help and understanding—just as the caterpillar did. Jesus wants us to help others and to be kind to them. If we make fun of others who goof up, we're like the badgers in our game. But if we help people and are kind, we're like the bunnies. Let's make cute caterpillars to remind ourselves to be kind to others who need our help.**

Hand each child a clothespin "butterfly body." Help kids glue squares of tissue paper (for wings) to the butterflies. Let kids use sequins and glitter glue to decorate their butterflies' wings. Then have kids use markers to add butterfly eyes and smiles!

Afterward, invite kids to "fly" their butterflies around the room.

Big Thank You (Veterans Day)

Best for early and upper elementary
Supplies: You'll need a Bible, markers, black and white newspaper pages, the comic section pages, and paper.

Form two groups and have teams stand on opposing sides of the room. Give one group a stack of black and white newspaper pages and the other group a stack of comic section pages. Have each group make a pile of paper wads.

On "go," have groups throw the paper wads back and forth at each other. The team that has thrown the most paper wads on the other team's side after one minute "wins."

Afterward, ask:
● How did it feel to have a pretend war?

● What do you think about real war?

● If you were asked to fight for our country, what would you do?

Have kids toss the paper wads away. Then say: **People in the Bible had to fight for their country often. But one time, the Israelites fought in a war and lost.**

Have kids act out the story as you read aloud Jeremiah 52:1-30. After the story, ask:

● Would you have liked to live in Jerusalem during this time? Explain.

● What would you have done if you had been captured?

● What freedoms do we enjoy in our country?

● How would our lives be different without these freedoms?

Say: **Many people have fought for our country to give us freedom to worship God and to live freely. Let's say thank you to the people who fought for our freedom.**

Hand children paper and markers and invite kids to create thank you cards for veterans. Deliver the cards to a veterans hospital or a Veterans Administration center to be distributed.

Calling All Friends! *(Back to School)*

Best for upper elementary
Supplies: You'll need children's Bibles, a long table, index cards, two toy telephones, and a marker.

Before class, write the following verse references on four index cards: Proverbs 17:17; John 15:12; John 15:13; and Philippians 2:4.

Put a toy telephone at each end of a long table. Ask a pair of kids to role play friends talking on the phone. Have partners decide who will be the first caller and who will be the first receiver. Read aloud the following situations and have a different pair role play the call each time.

● **Situation #1:** A friend calls to ask about the math assignment for tomorrow. Your friend goofed off in class and didn't listen to the directions and now is worried about getting the work done. What can you say to your friend?

● **Situation #2:** A friend has heard some gossip about you and wants to know the truth. Your friend isn't sure if the gossip was true. What do you say to your friend?

After the pretend phone calls, have kids form four groups. Hand each group a children's Bible and one of the index cards. Let each group look up its particular verse in the Bible then read it aloud for the entire class. Talk about the value of honest, open friendship. Then close in prayer, asking God to help the kids be good friends.

Caring Hearts *(Valentine's Day)*

Best for preschool
Supplies: You'll need a beach towel, red construction paper, tape, and scissors.

Before class, cut out a red construction paper heart for each child.

As children arrive, hand them the paper hearts. Say: **Be careful with the paper heart you have. We want to be gentle with our hearts. Can you carry your paper heart gently around the room?** Pause for children to respond. **Now give your paper heart a gentle hug.** Pause.

Spread a beach towel on the floor and place the paper hearts on the towel. Have the children hold the edges of the towel then gently bounce the towel up and down and back and forth to make the hearts move. Encourage children not to let any of the paper hearts fall.

Sit around the towel and say: **You were so careful with the paper hearts. Jesus is careful with our real hearts. Jesus loves us, and he takes good care of us. Let's wear these paper hearts to remind us how much Jesus loves us.** Tape the paper hearts to the children's clothing.

Catch the Gossip *(New Year's Day)*

Best for early and upper elementary
Supplies: You'll need a Bible, two rotating fans, masking tape, and a bag of shredded paper or paper confetti.

Before class, prepare a bag of shredded paper or purchase ready-made paper confetti. Then use masking tape to form a circle on the floor. The circle should be large enough for all the children to fit inside. Place two rotating fans outside the circle, positioned so they'll blow toward the kids.

Show kids the bag of shredded paper. Ask:

● **What is gossip?**

Say: **Let's pretend this shredded paper is gossip. When the wind blows, try to capture this gossip to keep it from spreading, but don't step out of the circle.**

Turn on the fans. Sprinkle the paper in front of the fans and encourage kids to grab it before it gets away. Remind kids not to step out of the circle.

After about 30 seconds, turn off the fans and have kids sit in the circle. Read aloud Proverbs 11:13 and 20:19. Ask:

● **How hard was it to capture the paper gossip?**
● **How hard is it to capture real gossip?**
● **What can we do instead of gossiping about people when we know a secret?**

Have kids help pick up and toss out the scattered paper bits.

Celebration of Love *(Easter)*

Best for early elementary
Supplies: You'll need margarine or butter, sugar, cocoa, water, vanilla, uncooked instant oatmeal, measuring cups, plastic bowls, spoons, powdered sugar, and party supplies such as party hats and noisemakers.

Set out the cookie ingredients, measuring cups, plastic bowls, and spoons. Invite kids to wash their hands then join in the fun of preparing a special no-bake celebration treat. Say: **Because Easter is such a special time, it's a time to celebrate. Let's celebrate by making delicious cookies.**

This recipe makes enough cookies for ten people. Cream ⅔ cup of margarine or butter. Stir in ¾ cup of sugar, 3 tablespoons of cocoa, 1 tablespoon of water, and ½ teaspoon of vanilla. Blend in 2 cups of uncooked instant oatmeal. Shape the mixture into small balls, then roll the balls in powdered sugar.

Hand out the cookies, party hats, and noisemakers and let kids celebrate Jesus' resurrection. Then lead children in singing this song to the tune of "If You're Happy and You Know It":

Jesus lives and you know it—
clap your hands!
Jesus lives and you know it—
clap your hands!
Jesus lives and you know it,
and your face will surely show it.
Jesus lives and you know it—
clap your hands!

Clap! Clap! *(Thanksgiving)*

Best for early elementary
Supplies: You'll need pastel construction paper and crayons.

Begin class time by singing a few songs to God and clapping after each song.
Say: **We just sang a few songs to God. What did we do after each song? We clapped our hands like this!** Give a few claps. **Clapping our hands after songs or movies is a way we can say "thank you." At Thanksgiving time,**

we want to tell God and other people thank you for all they do. Let's make special thank you cards.

Give each child a sheet of pastel construction paper and a few crayons. Have kids fold their papers to make cards. Then instruct each student to outline one hand on the front of the card and the other hand on the back.

Say: **At Thanksgiving, we thank God for all the things he has done. We can also thank other people for all the nice things they've done for us.**

Have kids decorate their hand prints to make them look like turkeys with colorful tail feathers. Have children sign their names on the inside of the cards. Encourage them to give their cards to friends or family members they're thankful for.

Eggstra Special Celebration *(Easter)*

Best for preschool through upper elementary
Supplies: You'll need a Bible, small individually wrapped candies, and two plastic pull-apart eggs for each child.

Before class, fill half the plastic pull-apart eggs with small individually wrapped candies. Leave the other half of the eggs empty. Be sure you keep the filled eggs and the empty eggs separated!

Gather kids in a circle and hand each child an empty egg. Invite children to open their eggs. Ask:

● **How did you feel when you found that the eggs were empty?**
● **Were you surprised when nothing was in the egg?**

Say: **Let's find out about a time when Jesus' friends found something empty.** Read aloud Mark 16:1-8. Ask:

● **Do you think Jesus' friends were unhappy that the tomb was empty? Why or why not?**

Say: **Jesus' friends were so happy when they found that Jesus was alive. It must have made them feel like having a party! Let's have a little party right now to celebrate the fact that Jesus is alive. We'll open more eggs for a fun surprise.** Hand the filled eggs to the children and have them open the eggs and enjoy the treats.

Family-Member Mobile *(Mother's Day/Father's Day)*

Best for early and upper elementary
Supplies: You'll need a Bible, construction paper, tape, scissors, yarn, markers, and coat hangers.

Set out the yarn, scissors, tape, markers, construction paper, and coat hangers. Invite kids to make representations of their family members out of construction paper then tape the paper people to lengths of yarn. Tape the yarn pieces of various lengths to the coat hangers to create mobiles. Encourage kids to hang the paper figures of the family members who live in their houses on one side of each coat hanger and family members who live elsewhere on the other side.

When everyone is finished with a mobile, encourage kids to talk about the people in their families.

Say: **Many families have family members who don't live in the same houses. Some family members may be away at school or living with friends. And some families have parents who are divorced and living in different places.** Ask:

● **What are some changes families may experience when they go through divorce?**

● **How do kids feel when their parents divorce?**

● **How can we help kids feel better when their parents divorce?**

Read aloud Romans 8:35-39. Ask:

● **What do these verses say about God's love?**

● **Can a divorce separate us from God's love? Why or why not?**

Say: **No matter what kind of changes divorce may bring, God will always be with us to comfort us and give us strength.**

Fishy Fun *(Summer)*

Best for preschool
Supplies: You'll need a Bible, fish-shaped crackers, construction paper, paper clips, scissors, small refrigerator magnets, string, tape, dowel rods or small tree branches, and blue fabric.

Before class, make a fishing pole for each child by tying a 3-foot length of string on the end of a dowel rod or a small tree branch. Wrap tape around the string to secure it to the "fishing pole." Tie a small refrigerator magnet on the end of the string as a "hook." Cut out a construction paper fish for each child and slip a paper clip on each fish. Make a "fishing pond" by placing a 3-foot circle of blue fabric (or construction paper) on the floor. Scatter the fish around the pond.

As kids arrive, invite them to go "fishing." Encourage kids to toss back the fish they catch so the fish can be caught again and again.

When everyone needs a break from this "fishy" activity, hand out fish-shaped crackers and let kids listen to one of the following Bible stories:

● Jesus calls the disciples to be fishers of men (Matthew 4:18-22),

● Peter's great catch of fish (Luke 5:1-11), or

● Jesus cooks breakfast for the disciples (John 21:1-14).

Friendship Flowers Bulletin Board *(Spring)*

Best for early and upper elementary
Supplies: You'll need green calico, brightly colored chenille wire, scissors, tape, paper muffin cups, construction paper, pencils, markers, a letter-size envelope, and a bulletin board or a bare wall.

Cover a bulletin board or a portion of the wall with green calico. Have kids use brightly colored chenille wire to form the words "Friendship Flowers." Then have them tape the words in an arch across the top of the display.

Have kids write their names on the inside bottom of paper muffin cups. Let kids tape the muffin cups all around the bulletin board so their names are facing out and can be read. Then have kids cut colored construction paper petals. Be sure each child cuts a petal for each muffin-cup "flower" on the bulletin board. Then invite kids to write affirmations on the petals for everyone in class. Suggest simple affirmations such as "You have a nice smile" or "I think you're a good friend." Have kids tape the affirmations in place around the appropriate muffin cups.

You may wish to provide a letter-size envelope with extra paper petals already cut out. Invite kids to add petals to the flowers each week. As the friendship flowers grow, so will love and good feelings among your kids!

Get Hoppin', Stop Poppin' *(New Year's Day)*

Best for early to upper elementary
Supplies: You'll need a Bible and balloons.

Before this activity, inflate a balloon for each child. Older children may enjoy inflating and tying off their own. Have the children sit in a circle.

Say: **Many people like to begin the new year with a fresh start, so they make resolutions, or decisions to change their behavior in some way. God wants us to begin each day with a fresh start, too. Let's listen to what God says about this in Ephesians 4:26.**

Read the Scripture verse aloud, then hand everyone a balloon. Say: **Raise** your hand if you've ever been angry. Can you show me your angry face? When I say "go," make your angriest face as you sit on your balloon and try to pop it.

Give the kids the signal and wait until all the balloons are popped, then ask:

● **What were you thinking as you popped your balloon?**
● **What's left of your balloon?**
● **What happens if we're mad at our friends for a long time?**

Say: **Let's listen to God's Word again.** Read Ephesians 4:26 aloud once more. **If we go to bed mad enough to "pop," we're often angry in the morning. God doesn't want us to go to bed angry. God wants us to ask for forgiveness from any person we've hurt. And God also wants us to forgive anyone who's made us mad enough to pop. When we get rid of our anger before we go to bed, we can have a fresh start in the morning.**

Let's pray. God, help us start each new day without anger. Remind us to forgive people who hurt us. Amen.

Have a Heart *(Valentine's Day)*

Best for preschool through upper elementary
Supplies: You'll need red or white construction paper, scissors, tape, a photograph of each child, a tree branch, a container filled with small rocks or marbles, chenille wire, and a hole punch.

February means Valentine's Day—a great time to help children share God's love with others! Here are a few fun, fast, and meaningful ways to share God's love in your classroom all month long.

● **Make coming into class fun.** Cover the outside of your door with red or white construction paper. Have children cut out heart shapes of all sizes and tape them to the door. Add the words "God is love" at the top of the door, using construction paper letters. Tape a photograph of each child on a heart to surprise the kids when they return.

● **Add a growing tree of hearts in your classroom.** Put a tree branch in a container filled with small rocks or marbles. Set out red and white construction paper, scissors, a hole punch, and chenille wire. Let kids create heart-shaped ornaments from construction paper. Have them punch a hole at the top of each paper heart then add a chenille wire "hook" to hang the heart from the tree branch. Have kids write on each heart one way God has loved them during the week and add it to the tree.

Healing Hearts *(Mother's Day/Father's Day)*

Best for early elementary
Supplies: You'll need red construction paper, scissors, plastic bandages, and markers.

Before class, cut a 5-inch red construction paper heart for each child.

Set out the plastic bandages. Gather kids in a circle and hand out the paper hearts. Say: **Sometimes moms and dads choose not to stay together. Some kids think their parents' divorces are their fault, and their hearts feel torn and hurt.** Have kids tear their paper hearts in half. **But it's not the kids' fault when parents divorce. It's because the parents decide they can't live together any longer.**

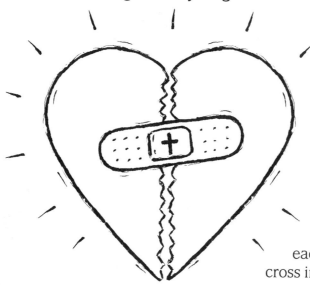

God knows it's sad when moms and dads leave each other in divorce. When parents can't live together anymore, our hearts feel like these hearts— all torn up and broken. We need powerful bandages of love to help our hearts heal. Only Jesus' love can make our hearts feel better.

Give each child a plastic bandage. Have kids "tape" their paper heart halves together. Let each child use a marker to draw a cross in the center of the plastic bandage.

Hosanna Parade *(Palm Sunday)*

Best for early elementary
Supplies: You'll need a Bible, scissors, rubber bands, and newsprint.

Let your kids experience the excitement of the first Palm Sunday with this involving activity.

Have children in each class make palm fronds out of newsprint. Use the following steps to make each frond:

1. Lay six sheets of newsprint in a pile.
2. Roll the pile of newsprint lengthwise to make a long "stem."
3. Fringe-cut the top edge of the stem. Gently twist the paper stem in a downward spiral while pulling upwards from the top of the middle of the stem to create floppy fronds and to lengthen the stem. Secure the bottom end of the stem with a rubber band.

When children have made their palm fronds, take children outside. Have them form two lines facing each other four feet apart. Have an adult dress up as Jesus and walk through the lines while children lay down their palm fronds as "Jesus" draws near so he can walk over them. Lead kids in singing praise songs such as "Hosanna."

When your hosanna parade is over, read aloud Luke 19:28-44.

I Can Do It! (Summer)

Best for early and upper elementary
Supplies: You'll need a Bible, a large bag of popped popcorn, and small paper cups.

Give each child a small paper cup. Toss a few popped popcorn kernels into the air and have each child hop on one foot and try to catch the popcorn with the cup. After a few tries, have the kids catch the popcorn in a different way, such as with one eye closed, by holding the cups in their teeth, or by moving backward.

Afterward, ask:
● **Did you catch much popcorn? Why or why not?**
● **How did you feel during this activity?**

Give the kids some fresh popcorn to nibble. Say: **Sometimes we may feel uncoordinated or clumsy when we can't do things as well as we'd like to. We may fall down when we run, or we may drop something we're carrying. Raise your hand if you know someone who does something better than you do.** Pause for responses. Say: **We all have things we can do really well and some things that we're not the best at. But that's all right— that's how God made us! Let's see what happened when Moses felt as if he couldn't do something right.**

Read aloud Exodus 4:1-17. Ask:
● **How did Moses feel about what God was asking him to do?**
● **What did Moses say to God?**
● **Why do you think Moses felt as if he wasn't good at doing things?**
● **What did God say to Moses?**

Say: **Moses felt awkward about what God wanted him to do. Moses didn't think he could do what God wanted. But God helped Moses understand that** not everyone is good at everything. God promised Moses his help—and God helped Moses all the way!

Inside Out *(Mother's Day/Father's Day)*

Best for upper elementary
Supplies: You'll need a Bible, index cards, a stapler, markers, and paper lunch sacks.

Hand each child an index card, a marker, and a paper lunch sack. Say: On the outside of your sack, write things that other people know about your family, such as how big your family is or what kind of house your family lives in. Then write on your card things that others may not know about you, such as things your family enjoys. Place the card inside your sack and staple it closed. People won't be able to get inside your sack unless you choose to let them in.

Allow time for children to finish their sacks and cards. Then ask:

● How does it feel to have family secrets that no one knows about?
● How are these sacks similar to the way families hide their problems?
● Who do you think knows all about our families and can help us?

Read aloud Psalm 139:16. Say: **God knows all there is to know about us. He knows us inside out, and he wants to help us—in good times and hard times, such as if our family goes through a divorce. God wants to help us with the things that are inside our sacks and in our homes. But we need to let him help us. Write "God" on the outside of your sack. Remember that you need to invite God to help you with any problems you may be having at home.**

Jesus Is Alive! *(Easter)*

Best for preschool
Supplies: none

Have children sit on the floor. Read this simple version of John 20:1-18: After Jesus died, Mary went to the cemetery early on Sunday morning to see where Jesus was buried. Other friends were there too. But when Mary got there, Jesus' body was gone. She was so sad that she cried. A man asked her why she was crying. She told him that Jesus had died and someone had taken away his body. Then she realized that the man was Jesus himself. Jesus was alive! She hurried away to tell her friends, "I saw the Lord!"

Ask the children to tell things that make them sad and happy. Emphasize that it's OK to feel sad about some things and to feel happy about other things. Let children describe ways they act or feel when they are sad or happy.

Say: **We can be happy at Easter time because God raised Jesus from the dead. And he is alive! Let's clap our hands to show how happy we are that Jesus is alive!** Lead children in clapping their hands for joy. Then invite children to suggest other ways to show they're happy, such as smiling, laughing, or hopping up and down.

Jesus Is the Light *(Halloween Alternative)*

Best for preschool
Supplies: You'll need a flashlight.

Gather kids in a circle. If possible, darken the room by lowering the window shades a bit. Hold the flashlight and ask:

● **What does this flashlight do?**
● **How can a flashlight make you feel safe when you're afraid?**

Say: There are many times we may feel afraid. Sometimes we're afraid of storms or animals or even the dark. But just as this flashlight helps us feel safe, Jesus helps us feel safe too. Jesus is like a big warm light! Let's play a fun game and sing a song. We'll stand in a circle and sing "Jesus Is the Light" to the tune of "The Farmer in the Dell." I'll shine the flashlight on each one of you in the circle. When the song ends, the person who has the light shining on him or her gets to shine the light as we sing again.

Lead the children in singing the following song to the tune of "The Farmer in the Dell."

Jesus is the light.
Jesus is the light.
Jesus is the light all right.
Jesus is the light.

Play until each child has been the flashlight holder.

Jumpin' Good Gifts *(Spring)*

Best for early elementary
Supplies: You'll need a Bible.

Tell children you're going to read some Bible verses from Psalm 65. Say: **Each time you hear me read something that God gives us, jump up and clap one time, then sit down.**

Read aloud Psalm 65:9-13. Children should be real "jumping beans" with these verses! After reading the portion of Scripture, ask:

● **How often did you jump up and clap?**
● **How many good things does God give us?**

Say: It's impossible to list all the wonderful things God gives us. But we know that the very best thing God gives us is Jesus. Jesus loves us so much that he died on the cross for us. And he rose from the dead so we can live forever. Now let's jump up one more time and clap to show how glad we are that Jesus is alive.

Leader Loyalty (Presidents' Day)

Best for early and upper elementary
Supplies: You'll need a Bible.

Choose someone to play the part of Moses. Say: **When we're loyal, it means we follow and obey. Let's show loyalty to our pretend Moses by following him and doing everything Moses says to do.**

Play Follow the Leader for one minute. Say: **Now it's time for a new leader. Moses, please choose someone to play the part of Joshua.** Pause while a new leader is chosen.

Say: **Before you lead the people, Joshua, let's hear what the Bible says about loyalty to a new leader.** Read aloud Joshua 1:16-18. Say: **God gave the people a new leader when Moses died. God appointed Joshua the leader, and the people were loyal to him. Let's show loyalty to our pretend Joshua by following him and doing everything Joshua says to do.** Play Follow the Leader for one minute.

Have kids form groups of three. Ask kids to talk about the following questions in their small groups. Ask the questions one at a time and allow about 30 seconds for the groups to discuss their answers. Then have groups share with the rest of the class what they talked about.

- **Why does God want us to be loyal to our country's leaders?**
- **Does God want us to obey leaders even if they're doing wrong things? Why or why not?**
- **Why do we want to be loyal to God first, then to our leaders?**

Close in prayer and ask God to help the country's leaders love God and be strong.

Light in the Darkness (Christmas)

Best for early and upper elementary
Supplies: You'll need a Bible and a flashlight.

Use this idea to involve children in worship with adults.

Have adults stand in groups of 10 or less, and secretly hand the flashlight to one of the adults. Encourage children not to run during this activity.

Say: **Before Jesus was born, people were in darkness.** (Dim or turn off the lights.) **But when Jesus was born, a light shone in the darkness to give people hope and to teach them about God.**

Let's pretend we're in the days before Jesus. Let's see if we can find the light of Jesus. When you find the light, say, "I've found the light!" One group has the light, but other groups may pretend to have the light.

Have kids walk around the room, looking for the light. Older children may hold the hands of younger children. Signal the person with the flashlight to turn on the light while other group members try to conceal it. Once kids discover the light, turn on the lights, gather the children together, and read John 1:1-5. Then ask:

● How did it feel to be in the darkness looking for the light?
● How did it feel when someone found the light?
● How do you think people felt when Jesus, the Light of the World, was born?

Let's remember that without Jesus, we'd be stumbling in darkness and wouldn't know God. Let's celebrate the light of Jesus with a song. Sing "Silent Night" or "The First Noel."

Like the Wind (Spring)

Best for preschool through upper elementary
Supplies: You'll need a Bible; a table; plastic drinking straws; a large fan or a hair dryer; and several lightweight objects such as feathers, facial tissues, leaves, and cotton balls.

Set the lightweight objects on a table and invite each child to choose an item. Give each student a plastic drinking straw and have children blow the lightweight objects around the room. Then turn on the fan or the hair dryer and blow several of the objects around the room. Encourage children to chase the objects and to catch them. When all the items are caught, have kids sit in a circle. Ask:

● Can you see the wind? Why or why not?
● How do you know the wind is there?
● Can you see God? Why or why not?
● How do you know God is there?

Say: **We can feel the wind and see what the wind does. In the same way, we can see God's presence in the way he takes care of us, in the way he answers prayers, and in his direction through the Bible. God is a spirit; he's invisible. That means we can't see him. But God is still there even though we can't see him.**

Read aloud John 3:8. Say: **I'm so glad that God is with us always. Let's pray and thank God for his presence. Dear God, thank you for being with us all the time. Help us know that you're always with us even though we can't see you. Amen.**

Living Valentines (Valentine's Day)

Best for early elementary
Supplies: You'll need a Bible and candy conversation hearts.

Hand each child a candy conversation heart. Say: **Turn to a partner and tell that person the message on your candy heart.** Pause for children to respond.

Say: **It's great to give each other special messages—you can even tell someone you love him or her through a special message. Eat your candy hearts while I read what the Bible says about another way we can show love to each other.** Read 1 John 3:18 aloud. Ask:

● What does this verse say about how to show love?
● How can we show love with our actions?
● Who could you show love to this week?

Say: **Let's practice some loving actions. Here are two more heart-shaped candies for each of you. Pass out the candies. Get with a partner. Then give one of your candies to your partner, along with a hug, and say, "Jesus loves you."** Then we'll get with new partners to give away the other candy hearts.

Loaves and Fishes *(Thanksgiving)*

Best for preschool
Supplies: You'll need a basket, a box of graham crackers, and a napkin or a small tea towel.

Before class, remove one cracker from the box of graham crackers. Prepare a picnic basket by placing the box of graham crackers in the bottom. Cover the box with a napkin or a small tea towel, then place one graham cracker on top of the napkin or towel.

Have kids sit in a circle. Show kids the graham cracker in the picnic basket and say: **Let's share this graham cracker while I tell you a story from the Bible about a boy who shared his lunch with a great crowd of people.** Paraphrase Matthew 14:14-19 as you break off tiny pieces of the graham cracker for the children to share. Be sure each child gets a piece of the cracker.

After the story, ask:
● **How did it feel to share one graham cracker with everyone else?**
● **How do you think the boy who shared his lunch felt?**
● **How did Jesus make the boy's lunch feed everyone?**

Say: **Jesus can do anything, and he fed that whole crowd with just five loaves of bread and two small fish.** Lift up the napkin in the picnic basket and say: **Oh! Look at all these other graham crackers! We have leftovers just as in the story. Let's share these graham crackers with everyone. But first we'll pray. Father, thank you for giving us food and everything we need. Amen.**

Hand each child a graham cracker to nibble.

Making God Happy *(Father's Day)*

Best for preschool
Supplies: You'll need a Bible, a trash can, yellow construction paper, white paper, tape, and crayons.

Help children learn what it means to make God happy by obeying him.

Before class, cut out a large yellow construction paper circle. Draw a simple happy face on the circle, then tape it to a trash can.

Give each child a sheet of white paper and a few crayons. Have each child draw a sad face on one side of the paper. Then on the other side of the paper, have each student draw a picture of something that makes his or her mom or dad sad, such as breaking something or yelling at a brother or sister.

When everyone is done, sit with children around the trash can with the happy face taped to the side. Say: **Things that make our parents sad also make God sad. God doesn't like it when we do wrong things or do things our parents tell us not to do. But when we tell God we're sorry about our mistakes, God is happy.**

Read aloud John 14:23-24. Ask:

● **What makes God sad?** Let kids hold up their pictures if they wish and tell about things that make their parents sad and things they think make God sad.

Say: **When we tell God and our parents that we're sorry for doing things that make them sad, we feel lots better! And it makes God happy when we ask for forgiveness. Now let's crumple the sad faces we drew and toss them into the trash can.**

Pray: **God, we're sorry that we do things that make you sad. And we're sorry when we do things that make our parents sad, too. Help us always make you happy. Amen.**

Miracles Happen (Easter)

Best for early and upper elementary
Supplies: You'll need a Bible, a large jar, a raw egg, a full container of salt, a long-handled spoon, and water.

Fill a large jar with water. Gather kids together, then gently drop the raw egg in the water. Say: **This egg really sank, didn't it? But we can make it float in the water. If you believe that we can make this egg float, put your hands over your hearts. If you're not sure that we can make the egg float, close your eyes.** Pause for responses. Then let each child stir salt into the water. Have kids keep adding salt until the egg rises to the top of the water.

Say: **Look—the egg is floating! We had faith that somehow the egg would float. Faith helps us believe even when we're not sure how something will turn out. Jesus wants us to have faith in him.** Read aloud Hebrews 11:1. Then ask:

● **How is the egg's rising like Jesus' rising from the tomb?**
● **Why is faith an important part of knowing that Jesus is alive?**
● **How can faith in God's miracles help us?**

Say: **Some things seem impossible, but God can do anything. Faith helps us know what our eyes can't see. And faith helps us know that Jesus is risen and is alive!** Challenge kids to share this fun "egg and salt devotion" with their families at home. Encourage them to talk about ways faith lets us know that Jesus is alive.

Mix It Up (Pentecost)

Best for early and upper elementary
Supplies: You'll need a Bible, prepared sugar cookie dough, chocolate chips, crushed peanuts, and a bowl.

Place prepared sugar cookie dough in a bowl. Set out the chocolate chips and crushed peanuts. Ask:

● **Who'd like to eat these ingredients?**

Say: **They may look good by themselves, but when they're mixed with other ingredients, they're even better!**

Read aloud 1 Corinthians 12:12-31. Say: **Just as good-tasting cookies have many ingredients, there are many ingredients that make up the church. Different people with their different talents and gifts mix together to make our church special.**

Find a partner. Then tell your partner one good ingredient he or she has that makes our church "taste better," such as a sweet smile or a great voice. Pause to give kids time to affirm each other. Ask:

● **What would happen if we left out an ingredient in a recipe?**

Say: **If we ignored some of the ingredients in a batch of cookies, the cookies might not taste so good. If we ignore people in our church, our church suffers. Now let's mix up a batch of great-tasting cookies!**

Have kids help stir the peanuts and chocolate chips into the cookie dough. Then scoop up a tablespoonful for each child. As you give each child his or her cookie dough, say, "I'm glad you're an ingredient in our church."

Music Message (Back to School)

Best for upper elementary
Supplies: You'll need a Bible, tape, newsprint, and markers.

Tape three sheets of newsprint to the wall. Write each of the following titles on a sheet of newsprint: "A singing group you like," "A singing group you don't like," and "Your favorite song."

Have kids form three groups, and hand each group a marker. Give the groups two minutes at each paper to write their answers under the title. Then have kids sit near the papers, and ask:

● **What makes you like a singing group?**
● **What kinds of messages does your favorite group sing?**
● **How can the messages we get from music affect how we feel?**

Ask a volunteer to read aloud Philippians 4:8. Have kids get back into their groups and evaluate their favorite and least favorite singing groups against each of the tests in this verse. Be sure to ask groups to report back to the entire class what they discovered.

Numbered Hair *(Thanksgiving)*

Best for preschool
Supplies: You'll need a doll with lots of hair.

Hold up the doll and say: **Let's see if we can count the number of hairs on this doll's head.** Begin counting aloud. When you get to 10, stumble over the numbers as if you've lost count.

Oh, dear! I got all mixed up and missed some hairs. Well, maybe we can count the hairs on (child's name) **head.** Choose a child with lots of long hair and start counting. Again, accidentally miscount.

This will never work! (Child's name) **has even more hair than my doll. We could count** (child's name) **hair for the next 10 years and not get the number right.**

Do you know how much God loves you? The Bible says God loves you so much that he knows exactly how many hairs are on your head. Think of that! That means when you wash your hair and six hairs fall out, God knows that, too.

Isn't it great to believe in a God who loves us so much? Let's tell God thank you for loving us. Fold your hands. Pray: **Dear God, thank you for loving us and for knowing everything about us—even the number of hairs on our heads. Amen.**

Partner Pairs *(Back to School)*

Best for early and upper elementary
Supplies: You'll need a men's large T-shirt, a wastebasket, and newspaper.

This activity makes a wonderful icebreaker for the first of the year.

Place newspaper at one end of the room and a wastebasket in the center of the room. Form pairs and have them line up on the side of the room opposite the newspaper. Hand the men's large T-shirt to the first pair in line and have both partners put on the T-shirt.

Say: **Let's play a game and see what it's like to help each other accomplish something. When I say "go," the first pair will rush to the newspaper. One partner will pick up a sheet of newspaper and crumple it. Then the other partner will take the newspaper and toss it in the wastebasket as the pair hurries back to the line. Then the next pair will go.**

As each pair makes a "basket," encourage everyone to cheer. When each pair has had a turn, ask:

● **What was easy about this race? difficult?**

● **How did you and your partner work together?**

Say: **It's important to help each other—even when we don't know the other person well. Jesus wants us to help everyone. And helping others is a good way to get to know them!**

Peer Choice (Back to School)

Best for upper elementary
Supplies: You'll need a Bible, pencils, and index cards.

Before class, prepare two index cards, each with one of the following situations:

● You're at school and you want to play football, but the kid who has a football is absent. Your friends tell you to take the ball from his locker. Decide which is the best choice:

    (a) you could take it because your friend would never know,

    (b) you could tell someone else to take it, or

    (c) you could suggest that the group play something else.

● While riding bikes, you and your friends begin to talk about smoking and drinking. They pressure you to smoke. Decide which is the best choice:

    (a) you could say, "Why ask me? Ask Bill to smoke instead."

    (b) you could say, "I don't want to try it" and then leave, or

    (c) you could try the cigarette then pass it on.

Gather kids and say: **Many times our closest friends have the strongest influence over us. Let's see how Jesus dealt with peer pressure from a close friend.**

Read aloud Matthew 16:21-23. Ask:

● **How did Jesus react when his close friend tried to persuade him not to go to Jerusalem and risk persecution?**

● **What might have happened had Jesus given in to Peter's peer pressure?**

● **What would the world be like today if Jesus had given in to peer pressure?**

Say: **Peter was trying to protect Jesus. However, people who keep us from doing what God wants us to do aren't good friends. We have choices to make in our friends and in how we act around our friends. Let's look at some choices.**

Have kids form two groups, and give each group an index card. If you have more than 15 kids, have kids form four groups and take turns reading the cards. Encourage each group to role play its situation with its chosen response then explain why it made that particular choice.

When each group has finished, say: **Pressure from friends can seem really strong. But Jesus is stronger. If we keep our eyes on Jesus and ask him to help us make good choices, we don't need to worry about peer pressure.**

Piles of Prayer Bulletin Board *(Fall)*

Best for early and upper elementary
Supplies: You'll need light blue wrapping paper; a small basket; tape; a small envelope; and orange, red, and yellow construction paper.

Before class, cover the bulletin board or an area of your wall with light blue wrapping paper.

Set out construction paper, tape, a small envelope, and the small basket.

Have kids tear interesting leaf shapes from orange, red, and yellow construction paper. Place the paper leaves and the tape in the basket and set the basket beside the bulletin board.

Write the title "Piles of Prayer" on a long strip of construction paper, then tape the title at the top of the bulletin board, tucking a few leaves behind it. On two smaller strips of construction paper, print the words "Concerns" and "Praises." Tape these papers at the bottom of the bulletin board.

Invite kids to write prayer requests on the paper leaves and tape them in a "pile" above "Concerns." Let kids write praises and thank you letters to

God on paper leaves and tape them in a "pile" above "Praises." Talk about the fact that God hears our prayers and answers in his time and way.

Encourage kids to each add a few leaves every week—and watch the piles of leaves grow!

Potter and the Clay *(Back to School)*

Best for early elementary
Supplies: You'll need a Bible, aluminum foil, a sheet of paper, a marker, and self-hardening clay.

Before this activity, tear off an 8-inch square of aluminum foil for each child. Build a small pot with a bit of the self-hardening clay. Make the pot look dilapidated. Also, write out Isaiah 64:8 on a sheet of paper.

Say: **The Bible says God is the potter and we are the clay.** Hold up the paper with Isaiah 64:8 written on it. Read aloud the verse and have the class repeat it after you. Then ask:

● **What do you think this verse means?**

Say: **If we allow others to mold us instead of letting God mold us, we may end up looking like this pot.** Hold up the dilapidated clay pot. **We** won't become who God wants us to be. The Bible warns us to stay away from doing wrong things. Friends sometimes want you to do wrong things such as disobeying your parents or cheating. You can learn to say no so you can do what's right.

Give each child a piece of self-hardening clay and a square of foil. Let kids form their own clay creations. Remind kids that as the "creators," they can make the clay into anything they like, just as God makes us into something he likes.

Have kids wrap their clay creations in the squares of aluminum foil and take them home. Tell kids their clay pieces will air-dry in a day or two.

Prayer Talk (Thanksgiving)

Best for early elementary
Supplies: You'll need a Bible, 20-inch lengths of string, paper clips, a pencil, and paper cups.

Give each child a paper cup. Tell kids they'll be making "telephones" together. Have kids form pairs, and hand each pair a 20-inch length of string and two paper clips. Have kids use the pencil to punch a small hole in the bottom of their cups. Thread one end of the string into the bottom of each cup, then tie the end of the string to a paper clip to anchor the string in the cup.

Have partners gently stretch out the string between them. Let partners take turns speaking in and listening through their "telephones."

After a few minutes, ask:
● How does it feel to talk to friends on the phone?
● How does it feel to talk to Jesus?

Say: **Talking on the phone can be fun, but we don't need phones to talk to Jesus. Prayer is how we talk to our best friend, Jesus. And he hears us any time and anyplace! I'm so thankful that Jesus hears us pray.**

Have the children stand in a circle. Read Philippians 4:6: **"Pray and ask God for everything you need, always giving thanks."** Have kids repeat the verse a few times in their pretend phones. Close with a prayer to Jesus, thanking him for being such a good friend who wants to talk to us.

Protector (Independence Day)

Best for early and upper elementary
Supplies: You'll need a Bible and newspaper.

Crumple three sheets of newspaper. Have kids form a circle with two volunteers in the middle. Designate one child in the middle as the "target" and the other child as the "protector." Hand the three newspaper wads to kids in the circle. Say: **Sometimes it's hard to feel protected and safe. In this game, the people in the circle will toss paper wads at the target. The**

protector will try to guard the target from being tagged by paper wads. If the target gets tagged, we'll choose a new protector and a new target to be in the center.

Play until every child has been in the center either as the protector or as the target.

Have kids sit down, then ask:

● Protectors, what made it difficult to guard the target?

● If you were a target, what was it like to rely on your protector?

Say: When people of a country guard the country and its leaders, that's called loyalty. Let's read about a country who was loyal to its king.

Read aloud 2 Samuel 18:1-7. Ask:

● Would you have this kind of loyalty to our country's leader? Why or why not?

● What helps you be loyal to our country?

● Who is always our best protector?

Play the game again if there's time.

T·I·P

For a festive treat after playing this game, serve ice cream cones and let kids sprinkle red, white, and blue candies over the ice cream cones.

Rainbow Promise (Spring)

Best for upper elementary
Supplies: You'll need a Bible; a ruler; a marker; scissors; cotton balls; tape; a roll of clear self-adhesive paper; and tissue paper in red, orange, yellow, green, and blue.

Before this activity, have kids cut 3-inch squares of colored tissue paper. Have them cut a large pile of paper squares! Keep each color in a separate pile.

Unwind a 3-foot length of clear self-adhesive paper on the floor. Keep the backing intact and be sure the clear side of the paper is facing up. Use a marker to divide the paper into five sections. Then remove the paper backing so the sticky side is facing up.

Let kids make a rainbow by pinching the center of each tissue paper square so the sides of the tissue paper "fan out." Stick the pinched tissue paper square to the self-adhesive paper. Fill each section of the "rainbow" with many pieces of tissue paper. Fill in any remaining areas of the sticky paper with cotton ball "clouds."

Hang the finished rainbow in a window and enjoy the effect as the sunshine streams through the colored paper. Gather kids by the rainbow and ask:

● How do you feel about the way we worked together?

● What would happen if everyone in the world cooperated instead of fought? Read Genesis 9:12-17. Explain that a covenant is a promise between two people.

Say: God made a promise to us. When he looks at a rainbow in the sky, he remembers that promise. Let's promise to work hard at cooperating with one another. When we look at our rainbow, we can remember our covenant—or agreement—with one another.

Have children say to one another, "I promise to cooperate with you." Then close in prayer.

Real Easter Eggs *(Easter)*

Best for early and upper elementary
Supplies: You'll need a Bible, seven plastic pull-apart eggs, a basket, a marker, thorns, toothpicks, a small sponge, vinegar, a 3×3-inch square of white fabric, a small stone, a cotton ball, and vanilla or cinnamon oil.

Before this activity, use a marker to number the plastic pull-apart eggs one through seven. Fill the appropriate eggs with the following items, then place the eggs in a basket.
- egg 1—thorns
- egg 2—two toothpicks
- egg 3—a small sponge soaked with vinegar
- egg 4—a 3×3-inch square of white fabric
- egg 5—a small stone
- egg 6—a cotton ball soaked with vanilla or cinnamon oil
- egg 7—an empty egg

Use your special Easter eggs to tell the story of the first Easter morning. Read aloud Matthew 27:29 and let kids open egg 1. Explain to the children that Jesus wore a crown of thorns when he died for us.

Read aloud Matthew 27:32 and have kids open egg 2. Lay the toothpicks in the shape of a cross.

Read aloud Matthew 27:48 and open egg 3. Let kids smell the vinegar, rub the sponge on their fingertips, and taste the vinegar.

Read aloud Matthew 27:59 and open egg 4. Explain that Jesus was covered with a white linen cloth and laid in the tomb.

Read aloud Matthew 27:60 and open egg 5. Let kids roll the small stone in their hands.

Read aloud Mark 16:1 and open egg 6. Explain that Mary and her friends brought spices to care for Jesus' body but found the empty tomb.

Finish the story by reading aloud Mark 16:6 and opening egg 7. Then ask:
- **Why is this egg empty?**

Say: **This is to remind us that the tomb was empty because Jesus is alive. Let's clap to show how happy we are that Jesus is alive!**

Right Costumes *(Halloween Alternative)*

Best for upper elementary
Supplies: You'll need butcher paper; markers; and art supplies such as feathers, yarn, sequins, and buttons.

Say: For Halloween, many people like to wear scary costumes. But as Christians, we know that the only thing we want to put on is God's love! Let's make costumes that remind us of God's love, his protective armor, or characters in the Bible.

Have kids form pairs. Have each partner lie down on a sheet of butcher paper while the other partner draws his or her outline. Let kids use the craft items to create biblical costumes or to illustrate the armor of God from the book of Ephesians.

After kids are finished, let them hold up their "costumes." Then gather kids in a circle. Go around the circle with each person praying, "Dear God, help me remember to put on my godly costume every day. Amen."

Sacrifice of Thanksgiving *(Thanksgiving)*

Best for early and upper elementary
Supplies: You'll need paper and markers.

Set aside a Wednesday evening or a Sunday morning before Thanksgiving to give children a special time to show their thanks. Two weeks before Thanksgiving, ask each child to think of one special thing he or she is thankful for. Send notes home to the parents, letting them know about this special Thanksgiving event and inviting them to attend.

One week in advance of your event, help the children make pictures or write poems about things they're thankful for.

During the Thanksgiving service, have the worship leader read Psalm 107:22. Invite children to come to the front of the church with their "thank you" offerings. Lead the congregation in singing "Come, Ye Thankful People" or "We Gather Together" as the children come forward.

Have the worship leader help children lay their "sacrifices" of thanksgiving on the altar or in an appropriate place. Invite the adults to join the children at the front of the church for a prayer of thanksgiving.

Brighten up the lives of shut-ins or nursing home residents by later giving them each one of the "sacrifices" the children have made.

Sharing Your Heart *(Valentine's Day)*

Best for early and upper elementary
Supplies: You'll need 8½×8½-inch sheets of red construction paper and a sheet of red poster board.

Give each child an 8½×8½-inch sheet of red construction paper as kids enter the classroom or worship area. You'll also need a sheet of red poster board that everyone can see.

Say: **Today we're going to use our red papers to tell a story about a girl who didn't get any Valentines at school. How do you think she felt?** Pause for responses. **This girl was so sad that she decided to take a walk in a large meadow with pretty red flowers.** (Hold up your poster board and encourage others to do as you do.) **She came to a small garden of red tulips. They were so pretty.** (Fold your poster board in half lengthwise and encourage kids to do the same.) **But the girl became sleepy and yawned. Can you yawn the way she might have?** Pause. **She was so sleepy that she decided to lie down for a little nap. It was cold, so she put some flowers over her as a blanket.** (Fold one bottom corner of the poster board upward.) **When she awoke, she saw an arrow.** (Fold the other bottom corner backward.) **The arrow was pointing to a bubbling, curving stream.** (Tear a rounded corner off the folded side of the top of the poster board.)

As she walked to the stream, she was excited and happy because she remembered something the Bible said: "This is what real love is: It is not

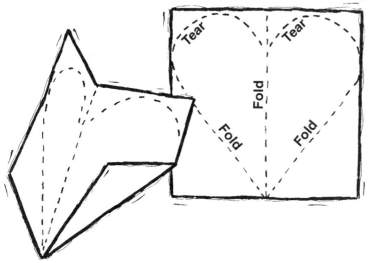

our love for God; it is God's love for us in sending his Son to be the way to take away our sins. Dear friends, if God loved us that much we also should love each other" (1 John 4:10-11).

The girl ran home and made Valentine hearts for all her friends. She wanted to share the great love God had given to her. (Open the poster board to reveal a heart shape.)

This Valentine's Day and every day, share God's love with as many people as possible. Now you can give your paper heart to someone you love.

Single-Minded *(Back to School)*

Best for early and upper elementary
Supplies: You'll need a Bible, string, and scissors.

Say: Today we're going to discover that we have the choice to stand up for what's right but that sometimes friends try to get us to do what's wrong. When friends try to get us to do something we don't want to do, that's called peer pressure. Let's play a game to see what it's like to do what your partner does.

Form pairs or trios. Gently tie partners together at the knees, using string. Tell children that this is a silent game—no talking allowed.

Call out the following commands and give children time to follow them:

● **Skip around the room backward.**
● **Hop up and down three times.**
● **Lie on your side.**
● **Trot around in a circle.**

Have children remain connected with the string while they answer the following questions.

● **How difficult was it to work together?**

Read aloud James 1:5-8. Ask:
● **What does it mean to be double-minded?**
● **How was this game like being double-minded?**
● **Is a double-minded person more or less likely to give in to peer pressure? Explain.**
● **According to James, how can we be single-minded?**
Say: **Having two brains working together is like being double-minded. There are two minds thinking two different things. Let's play the game again, but this time you can talk to your partner. Let's see what it's like to be single-minded.**
Play the game again, allowing children to talk.
Then ask:
● **Why was the game easier when you could talk?**
● **How was this like being single-minded?**
● **How can talking to God help us be single-minded?**
Reinforce this stand-up theme by leading kids in singing "The B-I-B-L-E."

Spiritual Wardrobe *(New Year's Day/Spring)*

Best for upper elementary
Supplies: You'll need a Bible, tape, markers, and newsprint.

Choose one of the kids to help you illustrate this message and ask this volunteer to stand before the group as you tape newsprint "clothing" onto him or her.

Say: **Let's make a list of things we do that make God unhappy. For example, God doesn't like lying, so I'll write "lying" on this costume. Each time you think of something, call it out then write it on the costume.**

When the children have covered the paper costume with their list, have another volunteer read the items on the list aloud to the entire group. Then read Ephesians 4:20-29 aloud.

Say: **The Bible tells us to take off the old self and put on the new self. God wants us to get rid of old things like greed and hate and being dishonest. Let's help** (child's name) **take off the costume of the old self.** Let the children rip off the paper clothing. Ask:
● **What does God mean when he tells us to put on the new self?**
● **How can God make us like new?**
Say: **The new self is just the opposite of the old self. For example, instead of stealing from people, the new self gives to people. Let's ask God to help us put on the new self.** Pray: **Dear God, thank you for this season of change as old things are made new again. Help us each to change the old self into one that pleases you. Amen.**

Spring-Fling Flowers *(Spring)*

Best for preschool to early elementary
Supplies: You'll need pretzel sticks; paper towels; and a variety of fruit such as pineapple chunks, apple slices, grapes, banana slices, and orange wedges.

Set out pretzel sticks, paper towels, and a variety of fruit. Invite kids to create delicious, fancy flowers from the fruits and the pretzels. Encourage kids to use a variety of fruits and to either connect the fruits using pretzel sticks or to lay the fruit pieces on the paper towels. You may wish to unroll a 3-foot length of paper towels on the table and have kids create a "cooperative garden" of goodies!

As you work, ask questions such as "What's your favorite part of spring?" and "Why do you think God gave us springtime and a season of newness?"

When kids have finished making flowers, say: **God gives us a new season of rebirth and newness each year. In spring, flowers grow, baby birds and animals are born, and everything is joyous and new. The Bible tells us that when we love Jesus and ask him to live in our hearts, we become new creations too. Let's say a prayer and thank God for the newness of spring and for our new life in Jesus.** Pray: **Dear God, thank you for giving us new things like flowers and baby birds. But thank you most of all for giving us new life in Jesus. Amen.**

Now let's gobble up our tasty flowers!

Stop-Look-Listen *(Back to School)*

Best for preschool
Supplies: You'll need scissors and red and green photocopies of the traffic sign from page 96.

Before class, photocopy on red construction paper the circle shape from page 96. Then photocopy another circle on green construction paper. Cut out the circles.

Hand the "stop" and "go" signs to two children. Say: **Let's pretend to drive cars. But we have to obey the traffic signs. Red means we stop. And green means we can go.** Let children "drive" their pretend vehicles around the room. Switch sign holders often. Play until each child has held a traffic sign.

Say: **Traffic signs are very important rules for drivers.** Ask:
● **What might happen if people didn't obey these rules?**
● **What are some rules God has given us?**
● **What might happen if we didn't obey God's rules?**

Say: **It's good to obey rules. We have rules to protect us, such as "Don't play in the street."** Ask:
● **What are some other rules that protect us?**

Say: **And we have rules to keep us from hurting others, such as "Don't tell a lie" and "Don't steal."** Ask:
● **What are some other rules that keep us from hurting others?**

Say: **Rules help keep us safe. It's important to obey rules.**

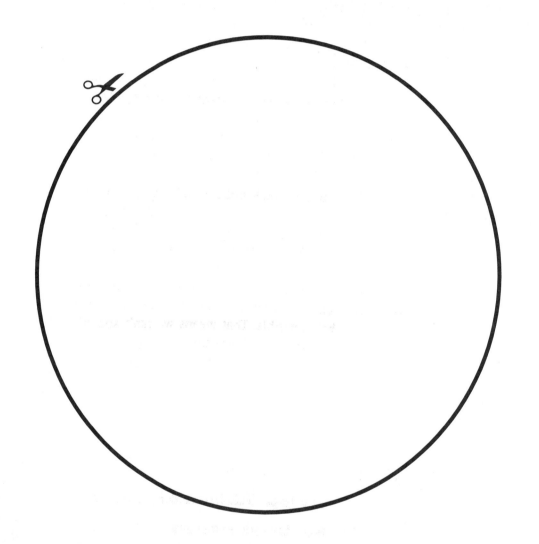

Surprise Package *(Christmas)*

Best for early and upper elementary
Supplies: You'll need a Bible, a large box, gift wrap, tape, scissors, a paper grocery sack, newspaper, a picture of baby Jesus, a small box, and a stapler.

Before class, gift-wrap one small box and one large box. Fill a paper grocery sack with newspaper and put the picture of baby Jesus on top of the paper. Staple the sack shut.

When children arrive, show them the two gift-wrapped packages and the paper sack. Say: **Part of the fun of getting presents is not knowing what's inside. What do you think is in these three gifts?**

Have children guess what might be in the packages. Then invite children to sit by the gift they'd like to open—but don't let them open the gifts yet. Ask:

● **Why did you choose to sit beside that package?**

Say: **Sometimes gift wrappings can surprise us.** Point to the sack. **A plain package might hold something very valuable. Today our story is about a gift that was from God and that came in a plain wrapper.**

Have the children remain where they are for the story. Tell the children to listen carefully for surprises in the story as you read aloud Luke 1:26-38 and Luke 2:1-20. Afterward, ask:

● **What unexpected events happened?**
● **Who was surprised?**

Have children give the thumbs-up or thumbs-down sign to indicate happy or unhappy surprises as you review these events from the story:

● An angel told Mary she would have a baby.
● Joseph and Mary took a trip when the baby was due.
● The inn was full when they got to Bethlehem.
● They found room in a stable.
● Angels announced Jesus' birth to the shepherds.
● God's Son came to earth as an ordinary baby.

Let the children open the three packages. Hold up the picture of Jesus. Say: **Sometimes great things come in plain wrappers. Jesus was God's happy surprise for the world!**

Team Spirit *(Flag Day)*

Best for preschool and early elementary
Supplies: You'll need white paper, drinking straws, tape, and red and blue crayons or markers.

Have children stand in a circle and hold hands. Have them walk to the center of the circle while saying "yay" and end with "team" when they meet in the center. Let kids do this several times. Then have the group work on a common goal such as straightening the room. Ask:

● **What do you like about being part of a team?**
● **How can teams and groups help each other?**

Say: **When we're on someone's team and we cheer for them no matter what, that's called loyalty. How do we show loyalty to our church? to God? to our country?**

Say: **Let's practice being loyal to our country by making our country's flag.**

Give children white paper and red and blue crayons or markers. Show them a picture of the United States flag and have them color their papers in red, white, and blue stars and stripes. Help children tape their flags to drinking straws so the flags may be waved in a march.

Say: **This month, we'll celebrate our country's freedom and our beautiful flag. We'll wave our flags and march around the room as I name good things about our country that we can thank God for. After I name each thing, wave your flags and shout, "Thank you, God!"**

Name things such as freedom to come to church, freedom to say what we think, and the privilege of going to school.

Thankful Place Mats *(Thanksgiving)*

Best for upper elementary
Supplies: You'll need a Bible, a table, colorful markers, wax paper, construction paper, scissors, magazines, newsprint, and an iron.

Set out markers, magazines, construction paper, and wax paper. Place the iron away from the kids and preheat the iron on medium heat.

Say: **Thanksgiving is a time to be thankful to God for all he's given. Let's make special place mats to remind you to have a spirit of thankfulness.**

Let kids each choose a sheet of construction paper to make a place mat. Help kids trim about half an inch from each side of their construction paper sheets. Read aloud 1 Thessalonians 5:18. Help kids write the words to 1 Thessalonians 5:18 on their construction paper sheets.

Invite kids to decorate the construction paper with cutouts from magazines and with colorful markers. Then help each child tear off two 8½×11-inch sheets of wax paper.

Lay several layers of newsprint on a table and set the iron on the table. One at a time, have kids bring you their decorated place mats and two sheets of wax paper. Layer each child's items as follows: one sheet of wax paper with waxed side up, construction paper with right side up, and wax paper with waxed side down. Cover the pile with several sheets of newsprint. Iron the newsprint evenly back and forth and check to make sure the wax paper is fusing to the construction paper. Let the place mats cool. Have kids take their place mats home, and remind them to thank God for his blessings daily.

Thanksgiving Feast Bulletin Board *(Thanksgiving)*

Best for early and upper elementary
Supplies: You'll need construction paper, scissors, and tape.

Your children can start now to make a difference for an inner city family at Thanksgiving time. For about $32 per family, kids can provide an entire meal, including a 10- to 12-pound turkey, two cans of vegetables, sweet potatoes, stuffing, cranberry sauce, a loaf of bread, fruit cocktail, a pie, and gospel literature.

Here's how your kids can be involved. Make a "Thanksgiving Feast" board and put it in a central place. Have your kids cut turkeys of different sizes out of construction paper and designate a dollar amount to each turkey size, such as $1, $5, or $10. Then have kids get to work. Kids can either contribute part of their allowance or organize fund-raisers to bring in money. Each Sunday, count the money given for turkey dinners and add the appropriate number of turkeys to your "Thanksgiving Feast" board. Once you reach $32, celebrate as a group that you've made a difference for a family who can't afford to have Thanksgiving dinner.

Thanksgiving Trees *(Thanksgiving)*

Best for early and upper elementary
Supplies: You'll need modeling dough, paper cups, a table, tree twigs, construction paper, tape, and markers.

Set the craft items on a table. Say: **Thanksgiving is a time to look at all that God has done for us and to give thanks. Today we're going to make thanksgiving trees that will continue to bloom with all the things we're thankful for.**
Have kids each "plant" a tree twig in a paper cup half filled with modeling dough. If you choose not to use dough, have each child simply turn the cup upside down and stick the twig down through the bottom of the cup. Have kids tear leaves from construction paper then draw or write things they're thankful for on the leaves. Tape the leaves on the twigs.
Have kids take their thanksgiving trees home, and encourage them to read the leaves with their families.

Thanks, God! *(Thanksgiving)*

Best for preschool and early elementary
Supplies: none

Say: **God has given us many good things—our eyes, our ears, our noses, our legs. Let's thank God for these things.** Read this story aloud to the children and have them do the accompanying actions.

Look! I see a bluebird. (Point up.)
Look! I see a brown squirrel. (Point in another direction.)
I'm glad God gave me eyes. (Point to your eyes.)
Up the hill we go, oh so slow (slap your thighs slowly)
And then run down fast. (Slap your thighs quickly.)
I'm glad God gave me legs. (Point to your legs.)
The tall grass swishes in the wind. (Slide the palms of your hands together.)
Listen to the sounds. (Hold your hand to your ear.)
I'm glad God gave me ears. (Point to your ears.)
Oh my, I smell a skunk. (Hold your nose.)
But oh, good—I smell a rose. (Take a deep breath.)
I'm glad God gave me a nose. (Point to your nose.)
Hooray! God gives us everything. (Clap your hands.)
I'm glad God gave me hands. (Hold up your hands.)
But I'm especially glad for cookies and milk. (Pretend to chew.)
Yum, yum, yum. (Rub your tummy.)
I'm glad God gave me my tongue. (Point to your tongue.)
Thanks, God, for everything. (Clap your hands.)

Thumb-Body Special *(Back to School)*

Best for preschool and early elementary
Supplies: You'll need construction paper, scissors, a ruler, a table, newspaper, damp paper towels, fine-tip markers, and colored washable ink pads.

Before class, cut 6×6-inch squares of construction paper. Be sure to use a variety of colors.

Cover a table with newspaper. Set out the construction paper squares, damp paper towels, and colored washable ink pads. Let each child

choose a construction paper square. Then let kids make thumb-print pictures by placing their thumbs on the colored ink pads and stamping their thumbs on the paper. Encourage kids to use various colors of ink and different fingertips for their prints.

Have children show their pictures when everyone is finished. Point out the differences in the prints' sizes, shapes, and colors.

Say: **God has made each of us special and different. You're old enough to choose what color of paint or paper to use. You can choose to do right things or wrong things, too. God wants you to choose to do right things—even if friends want you to do wrong things. When we make good choices, it makes God happy. Now let's draw happy faces on our thumb prints.** Have kids use fine-tip markers to add eyes, noses, and smiling mouths.

Time Capsule *(New Year's Day)*

Best for upper elementary
Supplies: You'll need cardboard tubes, paper, markers, pencils, aluminum foil, and rubber bands.

Take a trip into the future—make exciting time capsules to be opened in 10 years.

Set out paper, markers, pencils, and cardboard tubes from paper towel or bathroom tissue rolls. Invite kids to decorate cardboard "time capsules," using markers. As children work, direct their thinking toward things they'll do in the next 10 years and ways they can carry God's Word to other people in that time. Explain that God helps us make a difference in the world every day. Write a date 10 years in the future on each of the time capsules.

When kids are finished decorating the time capsules, have them write or draw pictures of ways they'll make a difference in the world in the next 10 years. Have kids slip their predictions into the time capsules. Wrap aluminum foil over the ends of the capsules, then secure the foil to the tubes with rubber bands. Store the time capsules in your church's attic, basement, or library.

Walk on Water (Spring)

Best for preschool
Supplies: You'll need two plastic-foam meat trays per child, pencils, scissors, and a large tub of water.

Give each child two plastic-foam meat trays. Have children place one foot on each tray and trace around their feet on their meat trays. Help children cut out their feet outlines. As you work, say: **Jesus did many wonderful and amazing things. One time Jesus even walked on the sea. He wanted to walk to his friends in their boat, so Jesus walked upon the water. Isn't that amazing?**

When the footprints are cut out, lead children to a large tub of water. Let children take turns floating their plastic-foam feet in the water. Say: **Our floating feet only pretend to walk on the water. Only Jesus can do anything. Take your fun feet home to remind you that Jesus can do anything!**

Who Is Your Guide? (Labor Day)

Best for early elementary
Supplies: You'll need chairs, tables, books, and wastebaskets.

Before this activity, set up an obstacle course, using books, tables, chairs, and wastebaskets.

Explain what kids must do to go through the obstacle course, such as climb over chairs, crawl under tables, or hop over books.

Have kids form pairs, and have each pair decide which partner will be the first leader and which will be the first guide. Let kids work their way through the obstacle course one at a time in a challenging way, such as walking backward, walking with closed eyes, or hopping on one leg. Have kids switch roles so each child has a turn as the leader and as the guide. Then gather kids together and ask:

● **What was the hardest part of this activity?**
● **How did it feel to have someone help you?**
● **How is this activity like having Jesus guide us through the obstacles in our lives?**

Say: **It's wonderful to know that we don't have to stumble and fall over every obstacle in our lives when we have Jesus as our guide!**

Wind Spirals *(Pentecost)*

Best for early and upper elementary

Supplies: You'll need a Bible, scissors, markers, ribbon, tape, construction paper, and access to a photocopy machine.

Before class, draw a spiral design on a sheet of paper then photocopy the pattern on a piece of construction paper for each child.

Set out markers, scissors, pencils, and ribbon. Hand each child a photocopy of the spiral pattern. Have kids cut the spirals along the outside edges and continue to cut in a circle until they reach the center of the spirals. Invite kids to decorate their wind spirals with ribbons and markers. Demonstrate how to hold a wind spiral from the center end so it "droops" down. Then let kids hold their spirals and gently blow on them to make them twist and turn.

Read aloud Acts 2:1-4. Then say: **After God raised Jesus from the dead, he sent the Holy Spirit on the day of Pentecost. There was a sound like the rushing of wind. Let's blow on our wind spirals.** Pause. **The Holy Spirit came like the rushing of wind. And just as we're helping our wind spirals move, the Holy Spirit helps put us into action for God. How does the Holy Spirit help you?** Pause for responses. **Tape your wind spirals up at home to remind you of the Holy Spirit's presence in your life.**

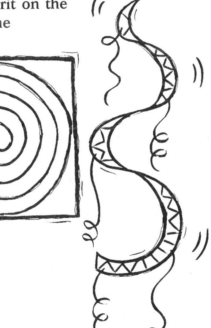

InDex

Best for Nursery
(Toddlers and 2-Year-Olds)

Best for Preschool
(3- to 5-Year-Olds)

Best for Early Elementary
(Kindergarten Through Third Grade)

Best for Upper Elementary
(Fourth Grade Through Sixth Grade)

● ●

Best for All Ages

Here's Practical Help for Your Ministry to Children!

Children's Ministry Magazine gives you **practical advice** on meeting the needs of smart kids...sweet kids...helpful kids...and kids who need a little extra attention, patience, and discipline. You'll learn the best way to **make a difference** with "challenging" youngsters—and their families—without having to disrupt the entire class.

We'll show you how to work with overachievers and underachievers. Kids who bounce happily into class and those who cry the first five minutes. Shy kids...latchkey kids...kids with disabilities...unchurched kids...kids whose personal worlds are crumbling...**you'll effectively share God's love and God's Word with them all—and we'll show you how!**

Here's what you'll find in every issue of *Children's Ministry Magazine*...
- 2 full pages of **"Keeping Current With Kids"**—the latest news and trends to keep you in touch with kids' changing world.
- **Group games** your kids will love to play.
- **"5-Minute Messages"** you'll have on hand to use on a moment's notice.
- **Seasonal ideas** you'll use to plan ahead—PLUS exciting holiday ideas you can use immediately.
- 12 big pages of **"Ideas You Can Use"** with everything from community-building to encouraging deeper faith in kids.
- In **"Age-Level Insights"** you'll get helpful glimpses into the way your kids think...listen...feel...and know how to best reach them!
- **Photocopiable pages** of priceless pointers for teachers and parents!
- Valuable **Volunteer Helps**—so recruiting, training, and hanging onto volunteers will be a snap!

All this for the special introductory price of just $19.95 for one year (6 issues)—a 33% savings off the cover price!

Order your first issue today...you'll find dozens of ideas that will make your job easier!
Call toll-FREE...
1-800-877-6143

**The Most Widely Read Resource
for Those Who Work With Children in the Church**

Ask for offer No. A6111C